A History of
Watercolor

A History of
Watercolor

Bernard Brett

EXCALIBUR BOOKS
NEW YORK

Photographic acknowledgements
The pictures on pages 68 right, 94, 100 and 166 are reproduced by gracious permission
of Her Majesty Queen Elizabeth II; the pictures on pages 132, 151, 161 top and 172
are reproduced by permission of the Syndics of the Fitzwilliam Museum, Cambridge;
and the picture on page 135 bottom is reproduced by courtesy of the Cotman Family.
©ADAGP 1984 235 bottom, 236, 237 top, 237 bottom, 238, 242 top, 248 top, 248
bottom; The Art Institute of Chicago 158, 198 bottom left; Ashmolean Museum,
Oxford 74-75, 115, 122-123, 171 top; The Board of Trinity College, Dublin 48, 49,
50, 51; The Bridgeman Art Library, London 35, 36, 37, 38, 40, 41, 42, 43, 44, 46, 58,
63, 66, 67 top, 67 bottom, 68 left, 69, 70, 71, 77, 79, 87, 95, 98, 102, 105, 107 top,
108-109, 112 bottom, 114, 124 top, 124 bottom, 125, 126, 128-129, 133, 143, 148,
155, 159, 160 top, 162 top, 162 bottom, 167 top, 169, 173, 174, 175 top, 181, 186,
187, 197, 207 top, 212 right, 213, 230 bottom, 237 bottom, 239 right, 241, 242 top,
243; The British Museum, London 27, 78, 80 top, 81, 82-83, 84, 88, 89, 92, 96-97,
104, 110, 111, 116-117, 118 top, 118 bottom, 120-121, 122 bottom, 127 bottom,
130-131, 134, 139, 141, 142, 150 top, 152, 165 bottom, 210, 211, 212 left; Ets J E
Bulloz, Paris 225; Columbus Museum of Art, Ohio 199; The Cocoran Gallery of Art,
Washington, D.C. 190 top, 192, 196 top, 196 bottom, 198 top, 198 bottom right,
200 bottom, 250 bottom, 251 top, 251 bottom; © DACS 1984 231 right, 232-233,
234, 235 top left, 235 top right; Mike Davis Studios Ltd, London 216; Mary Evans
Picture Library, London 17, 18; Freer Gallery of Art, Smithsonian Institution,
Washington, D.C. 190 bottom, 191 bottom; Hamlyn Group Picture Library, Feltham
21, 22, 25, 39, 52, 54, 72, 73 left, 73 right, 76 left, 76 right, 229 bottom; Michael
Holford, Loughton 23, 24, 26; Imperial War Museum, London 204-205, 205 top, 207
bottom; Laing Art Gallery, Newcastle-upon-Tyne 106; Leeds Art Galleries 119; The
Metropolitan Museum of Art, New York 193 top, 193 bottom, 194, 195 top; Museum
of Fine Art, Boston 191 top, 195 bottom; National Gallery of Art, Washington, D.C.
201 top, 201 bottom, 248 top; National Gallery of Ireland, Dublin 230 top; National
Galleries of Scotland, Edinburgh 140; National Maritime Museum, London 175
bottom, 183 top, 184; National Museum of American Art, Smithsonian Institution,
Washington, D.C. 246, 249, 250 top; Peter Newark's Western Americana, Bath 188
bottom left, 188 bottom right, 189; Norfolk Museums Service, Norwich 135 top, 136
top, 136 bottom, 137, 138; Michael Petts 13; The Phillips Collection, Washington,
D.C. 200 top; Photographic Giraudon, Paris 62 top, 62 bottom; Rowney & Co Ltd,
London 16; Royal Geographical Society, London 176-177; Scala, Antella 28, 29, 30,
31, 32-33, 34, 56-57, 59, 60-61, 62 top, 64-65; Scott Polar Research Institute,
Cambridge 178; The Tate Gallery, London 152-153, 154, 156-157, 161 bottom, 164
top, 164 bottom, 170, 171 bottom, 179, 180, 202-203, 206, 208, 209, 236, 239 left,
240, 242 bottom, 244-245, 247; Theatre Museum, Victoria and Albert Museum,
London 214, 215, 217; Victoria and Albert Museum, London, Crown Copyright 85,
112 top, 113, 127 top, 144, 145, 149, 160 bottom, 165 top, 167 bottom, 168; Walker
Art Gallery, Liverpool 182; Whitworth Art Gallery, University of Manchester 80
bottom, 107 bottom, 183 bottom, 185; Yale Center for British Art, Paul Mellon
Collection, New Haven 86, 91, 103, 146-147, 150 bottom; Joseph P Ziolo, Paris: Faillet
19, 220, 226, 227, 228, 229 top; André Held 218, 218-219, 221, 222, 224, 231 right,
232-233, 235 top left, 235 top right, 235 bottom, 237 bottom, 238, 248 bottom; Ph
Nimatallah 234; Oronoz 20; René Percheron 231 left.

Front cover: *Woman Sewing,* Winslow Homer. In the Collection of the Corcoran
          Gallery of Art, Washington D.C. Bequest of James Parmelee. (24.8 ×
          20 cm/9¾ × 7⅞ in). Cover reproduction has been enlarged from the
          original.
Back cover: *Jacob's Ladder,* William Blake (British Museum, London).
Title page: *Highgate from Upper Holloway,* John Absolon. In the Guildhall
          Library, City of London (The Bridgeman Art Library).

First published in the USA 1984
by Excalibur Books
Distributed by Bookthrift
Excalibur is a trademark of Bookthrift Marketing, Inc.
Bookthrift is a registered trademark of Bookthrift Marketing Inc.
New York, New York

Prepared by
The Hamlyn Publishing Group Limited
Bridge House, Twickenham, Middlesex, TW1 3SB, England

Copyright © 1984 by The Hamlyn Publishing Group Limited
Reprinted 1987
For copyright reasons this edition is only for sale
within the USA.

ISBN 0-671-80797-8

Printed in Hong Kong by Mandarin Offset

Contents

Introduction

Most of us first came across watercolour as infants in the nursery and made some of our earliest attempts to express ourselves visually in that medium. It seems only natural that those whose practical interest in painting survives that stage should continue to use it.

The word itself is confusing. 'Watercolour' may refer to any pigment, or colour, which is diluted with water and applied to a surface with – normally – a brush; it may be the paint itself, or it may be a description of a certain technique in painting – watercolour as opposed to oil painting (the medium of the Old Masters). This book sets out to explore the history of the medium in the widest possible sense, tracing the use of water-bound paint for a more or less 'artistic' purpose from the time of the cave artists of Lascaux and Altamira up to the experimental work of practitioners at work today. Since oil painting was not known before the Renaissance, the art of the ancient Egyptians, the Greeks and Romans and the early Middle Eastern societies is all part of the story. In Europe, however, watercolour was largely neglected as a medium, except for miniatures (which sprang from the illuminated manuscripts of the Middle Ages) throughout the 16th, 17th and early 18th centuries.

In the Far East things were very different. The painters of China and Japan used water-based paints on paper and silk to produce images of the highest sophistication, though of a form generally alien to the European artistic tradition.

But, when we speak in general terms of watercolour painting we are thinking, above all, of its development in England in the 18th century, when it was linked with the growing interest in topography and landscape. This is the 'true' watercolour, pigments bound with gum and diluted with water to produce colours that are, unlike tempera or gouache, or of course oils, transparent. At first it was a matter of tinting pen drawings with sepia or blue; that gave way to monochrome painting, which in turn was superseded by the broad, confident handling of washes of brilliant colour to achieve masterpieces of atmosphere.

It is usually assumed that watercolour, the common medium of weekend artists, is easier to handle than oil paint. In many ways this is true, and it is not only simpler, it is a great deal cheaper! But the fact that the amateur painter finds watercolour a simpler proposition does not mean that it is any easier to produce a masterpiece in watercolour than it is in oils. To exploit the freshness and light which are the special virtues of the medium demands a sureness and spontaneity that are not acquired easily, if at all.

The art of pure watercolour consists of glazing transparent colours one upon the other in the thinnest of layers, allowing the paper itself to act as a lighting agent. The age-old maxim, 'Never lose your paper', remains an infallible guide to the aspiring watercolourist. The luminous brilliance is enhanced by the granulation of the paper: the hollows, being loaded with paint, give a depth and richness of colour in contrast to the reflective lustre of the raised surfaces.

The oldest method of painting in watercolour is *a fresco*. In this technique the paint is applied directly to damp, fresh (*fresco*) plaster, which sucks in the colour and calcifies it into a rock-hard amalgam. This was in fact the technique of the hunter artists of Altamira, though acquired entirely by chance and of course with no knowledge of its significance. Later, a greater richness was obtained by binding pigments with yolk of egg and diluting the resulting emulsion with water; this method, known as tempera, was widely used in the Middle Ages. Gouache is an opaque form of watercolour achieved by mixing white with the original pigment. The Chinese used gouache to great effect thanks to a white pigment ground from seashells. Nowadays, coloured inks produced from synthetic dyes give a greater intensity of colour, but most of them tend to be 'fugitive' – rapidly fading in sunlight.

Many of the world's greatest artists have turned to watercolour not only to make quick sketches or studies for future oil paintings but to create finished works of art that cannot be dismissed as in any way inferior to works in the more conventional medium of oil paint. Cézanne, after all, whose significance for the whole of modern art seems to grow with the passing years, frequently and enthusiastically worked in watercolour. Nevertheless, it is above all the great masters of the English landscape in the late 18th and 19th centuries who demonstrated the brilliance and subtlety of watercolour painting.

1
Colour and Pigments

White light, when passed through a prism, breaks down into its component parts, wavelengths of radiant energy that go to make up the familiar rainbow spectrum. It is the action of selective wavelengths of this radiant energy on the mechanism of the eye that allows us to see a particular colour. Light falling for instance on a primary red surface reflects only the wavelengths that give a sensation of pure red, while those at the blue/yellow end of the spectrum are absorbed. A crimson surface, however, reflects some blue rays as well as the primary red ones, causing us to see a bluish red. This optical law applies to all pigments and dyes, the specific behaviour varying from colour to colour.

In theory, it would seem, any chromatic hue can be obtained by mixing a combination of the three primary colours, red, yellow and blue, but in practice only an approximate hue can be gained by mixing 'pigmented' colour. A watercolour palette embracing a further selection of ready-mixed pigments is required if the artist is to work in bright, clean colours. As watercolours are transparent or semi-transparent, one colour can be glazed over another to effect a change of hue. However, with each layer of colour the interaction of reflection and absorption becomes more complex, and the luminosity and freshness of the colour is decreased.

As far as we know the earliest painters had only four or five simple colours; white, yellow and red ochres, brown and black. Later, the Egyptians, then the Romans, extended this limited palette into a rich range of brilliant colours obtained from both mineral and vegetable sources. Over the centuries this range has steadily grown, and for that matter is still growing, as artist and artist's colourman constantly add to the list of available colours. Nowadays the watercolour artist can choose from over one hundred different colours, all conveniently presented in pans, cakes and tubes.

There is more to making a watercolour paint than simply mixing pigment with water. To ensure that the paint adheres to the paper and does not flake off when dry, it is essential to add a binding agent. All manner of ingredients have been mixed with pigments to provide such a vehicle – rice paste, flour, animal size, even casein of cheese – but the most successful have been a variety of gums: gum arabic, tragacanth, fish glue and numerous others. In the past, when artists ground their own colours, each had a favoured binding agent – possibly with a secret ingredient that he believed gave him the edge over his fellow artists.

In practice today's artist's colourman binds the powdered pigment with gum arabic, adding honey and sugar to counteract the brittleness of the gum and glycerine to keep the paint moist; this is particularly important in preparing the moist colours presented in tubes. Although gum arabic dissolves readily in water, enough remains to act as a thin varnish which increases the luminosity of the colour. To accelerate drying, the 18th-century watercolourists often added spirit to their water; a drop of brandy or whisky was usually preferred, although Paul Sandby favoured gin.

Some pigments are permanent and retain their brilliance, others

PRISMATIC

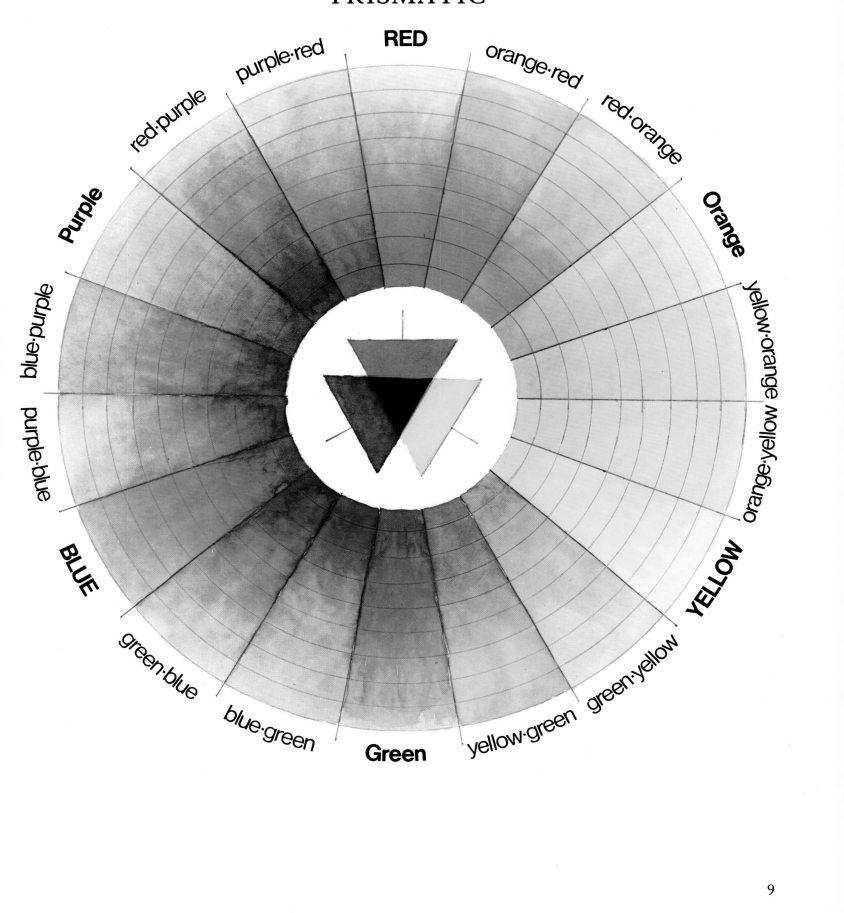

RED

purple·red

orange·red

red·purple

red·orange

Purple

Orange

blue·purple

yellow·orange

purple·blue

orange·yellow

BLUE

YELLOW

green·blue

green·yellow

blue·green

yellow·green

Green

fade in sunlight and are classed as fugitive. The modern artist's colourman usually grades colours, according to their durability, as permanent, durable, moderately durable or fugitive colours. One artist's colourman gives this definition of permanence. 'By permanence of a Water Colour we mean its durability when washed on Whatman paper and exposed freely, under a glass frame in a dry room, for a number of years, to ordinary daylight: no special precaution (other than the usual pasting of the back of the frame) being taken to prevent access of an ordinary town atmosphere. . .'

Although it is difficult for an adventurous colourist to work solely within the range of the permanent colours, it is nevertheless advisable to restrict the palette to less, rather than more colours. As early as the turn of the 19th century, Edward Dayes was writing: 'one great inconvenience the student labours under arises from the too great quantity of colours put into his hands; an evil encouraged by drawing master and colourman. . . [It] is not uncommon to give two or three dozen colours in a box, a thing unnecessary.' David Cox, in *A Series of Progressive Lessons in Water-Colours* (1816), suggests this palette:

Gamboge	Vermilion	Indigo
Light ochre	Burnt Sienna	Black
Light red	Vandyke brown	Sepia
Lake	Prussian blue	

A contemporary of Cox recommended this palette:

Light Oker	Light Red	Indigo
Orange Orpiment	Red Lead	Burnt Terra di Sienna
Raw Terra di Sienna	Lake	Vandyke Brown
Gamboge	Prussian Blue	Cologn Earth
	Indian Ink	

It is interesting to compare these with the list of colours Ralph Mayer suggests watercolourists should choose from in his *Artist's Handbook of Materials and Techniques* (1940).

Whites	Titanium (permanent)
	Chinese (permanent)
Blacks	Ivory, lamp black (permanent)
	Mars black (permanent)
Reds	Light, medium, dark cadmium (durable)
	Alizarin (durable)
	Iron oxides, Mars, Venice, Indian red (permanent)
Yellows	Light, medium, dark, orange cadmium (permanent)
	Mars and ochre yellows (permanent)
	Raw sienna (permanent)
	Aureolin (permanent)
	Strontium and barium yellow (durable)
Blues	Ultramarine (permanent)
	True cobalt (permanent)
	Cerulean (permanent)
Greens	Emerald (permanent)
	Oxide of chromium (permanent)
	Green earth (permanent)
	Cobalt, turquoise, ultramarine green (permanent)
Violets	Cobalt and manganese violet (permanent)
	Violet alizarin (permanent)
	Mars violet (durable)
Browns	Raw and burnt umber (permanent)
	Burnt sienna (permanent)
	Brown alizarin (permanent)
	Burnt green earth (permanent)

COMPOUND

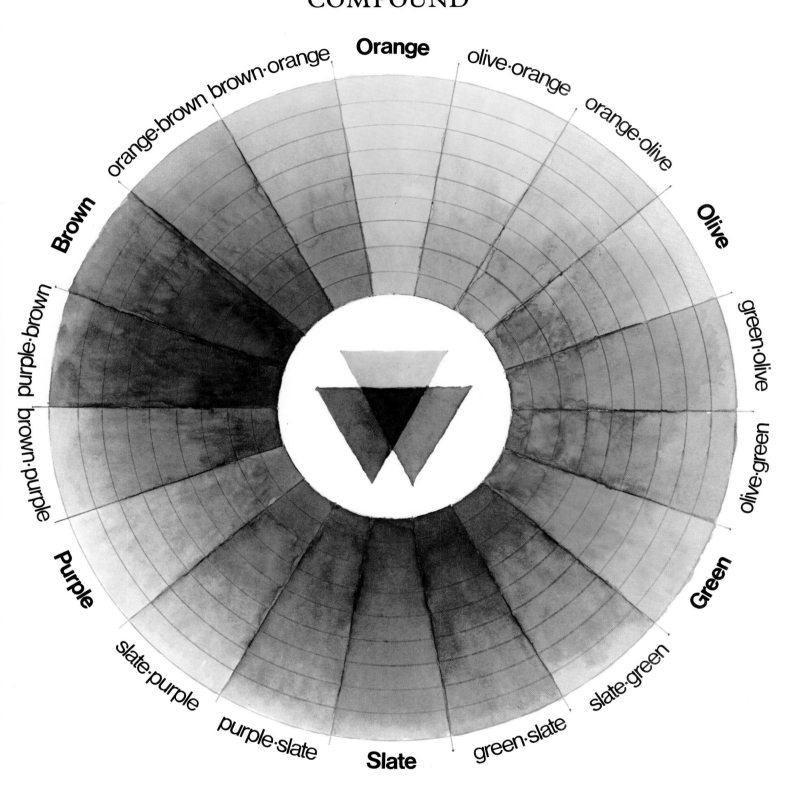

Orange

olive·orange

brown·orange

orange·brown

orange·olive

Olive

Brown

green·olive

purple·brown

olive·green

brown·purple

Green

Purple

slate·green

slate·purple

green·slate

purple·slate

green·slate

Slate

11

2

Paper

Choice of paper is of major importance in watercolour painting and every great watercolourist has had his favourite. Some have preferred a heavy, or thick paper, some a light, or thin paper. (The thickness of paper is determined by the weight of a ream, and ranges from 72 lb (32.7 kg) to the heaviest 400 lb (181 kg) pasteless boards.) Some artists have preferred a smooth surface, some a rough one. The best-quality watercolour papers, hand-made from white linen rags, are immensely superior to machine-made papers produced from cotton fibre or wood pulp. Linen papers take washes well and withstand rough treatment; colour on them has a brilliant fresh appearance. Cotton papers are difficult to moisten and unsuitable for washes; colour on them appears dull and lifeless. Those made from wood pulp preclude all depth of tone and in a short time turn yellow and brittle.

Good-quality hand-made papers are made in varying weights and are supplied with three types of surface, 'hot-pressed', 'not', and 'rough'.

The term 'hot-pressed' is misleading, as no heat is used in the process of glazing the surface; this is done by subjecting each sheet to a pressure of several tons to the square inch. Although smooth, with very little grain, there is enough texture to accept a wash.

A 'not' (i.e. not pressed) surface has a medium grain, halfway between smooth and rough. Less pressure is applied to achieve this grain, which readily controls a wash and is probably the most popular texture with watercolour artists.

As its name implies, 'rough' paper has a heavy grain, which assists evenly controlled washes. No pressure is applied in its manufacture; the sheets are simply stacked one upon the other and left under their own weight for several weeks until they become sufficiently flat.

The labour-intensive process of producing one sheet at a time makes hand-made papers very expensive. However, mould-made papers, of good quality though made by machine, are an adequate substitute and are certainly much cheaper.

Genuine hand-made papers, with uncut, deckled edges, can easily be identified by their watermarks. They are made by a craft process that has hardly changed since the 18th century, a craft rich in traditional names and expressions. After the white linen rags have been carefully sorted, they are pulped in the 'beater', bleached, run into 'stuff chests' and cleaned in spring water until free of all starch and dirt before being transferred to the vats. The mould (consisting of a removable wooden frame or deckle enclosing a woven wire cloth which carries the design of the manufacturer's watermark) is dipped into the vat and filled with enough pulp to make one sheet of paper. A deft shake by the vatman assists the 'felting' of the fibres. The mould is passed to the 'coucher' and pressed down on to a rough blanket or felt, to which the viscose paper pulp adheres. The empty mould is then refilled by the vatman and the process is repeated. When there is a sufficiently high stack of moist paper, interleaved between felts, it is fed into a hydraulic press and the excess water squeezed out. At this point the paper takes on the distinctive grain of the felt.

Opposite: A selection of watercolour papers: 1. RWS 90; 2. Green's Pasteless; 3. Whatman's Rough 200; 4. Fabriano NOT 90; 5. Whatman's HP 140; 6. Ingres; 7. Bockingford.

It is now known as 'water leaf' or 'plate paper' and has almost the absorbency of blotting paper. This is passed through a trough of animal glue or gelatine size, excess glue being squeezed out by rollers, and the sheets are hung up, steamed and dried for forty-eight hours at a controlled temperature. Sizing is essential to ensure that the paper accepts a wash evenly, without spreading.

Not all watercolour papers are white. A number are tinted, or have a mottled tone. In 1836, David Cox began to use a special paper (produced today under the name David Cox paper), which he came across quite by chance. It was a coarse, heavy wrapping paper manufactured at a paper mill in Dundee. Made from old, bleached sailcloth, ropes, sacking and other rags, it had a warm, greyish tinge and was flecked with specks of brown and black. Being only lightly sized, it absorbed colour more easily than the then fashionable Whatman papers, the hot-pressed version of which had to be well soaked to prevent colour lying on the surface, creating hard edges to the washes. It was the use of this Scottish wrapping paper which enabled David Cox, in his later work, to achieve his characteristic soft edges. Peter de Wint also preferred wrapping paper; his was oatmeal in colour and had a coarser texture than that of David Cox. A modern version of this paper can also be bought today.

The following papers are used by watercolourists nowadays.

Hand-made papers. David Cox paper: a tinted paper with a speckled surface; a modern version, with the same character and qualities, as that used by Cox.

Cotman paper: white, with a more even texture.

Crisbrook paper: a coarse-textured paper, tinted oatmeal.

De Wint paper: oatmeal in colour, a modern version of de Wint's wrapping paper.

Green's pasteless board: a heavy white board, between 200 and 400 lb (90–180 kg).

RWS paper: white, 72 to 140 lb (32–63 kg).

Saunders hand-made: white, 44 to 240 lb (20–109 kg).

Mould-made papers. Fabriano papers: good-quality Italian papers, white and tinted.

Bockingford paper: very absorbent white paper, 90 to 140 lb (40–63 kg).

Saunders mould-made paper: white, 44 to 240 lb (20–109 kg).

Hollingworth Kent cartridge paper: good-quality white cartridge paper, 90 to 185 lb (40–84 kg).

Ingres paper: French and Italian papers in various tints, 33 lb (15 kg).

3

Brushes

The use of brushes in painting dates back to Paleolithic times. Judging from the quality of the work in the caves at Lascaux, Cro-Magnon man used crude brushes, probably made from animal hair, feathers, reeds, or even moss. Certainly the Egyptians and the Romans had very efficient brushes, made in much the same style as they are today. From the 15th to the mid-19th century watercolour brushes were known as pencils; indeed, Chaucer refers to the 'subtil pensil'. A 17th-century writer gave this advice on their selection. 'Your next care must be to provide yourselfe with god pencills well chosen, clean and sharppe pointed, not dividing into two parts as many times they doe nor stufft with stragling heires, which later you may take away with a sharpe penknife or by passing the pencill through the flame of a Candell. The best are of reasonable length, full, round and sharpe, not too longe, nor too slender, which are troublesome to work with'.

This advice still holds good today; a perfect watercolour brush should be thick near the ferrule, tapering to a fine point – never short and stubby. Yet some great watercolourists broke this cardinal rule. Peter de Wint often limited himself to two favourite brushes, one fine, the other thick and stubby, and Samuel Palmer was occasionally known to use a brush two inches broad.

Although one large red sable brush, a number ten or twelve, will do the finest or broadest work, most watercolour artists use three or four different-sized brushes, though never too small. As James Roberts wrote in 1809, 'With respect to camel's hair pencils, the larger and largest sort should be procured, and chiefly used: very small camel's hair pencils will in time give the student a "petite" manner.'

Until the middle of the 19th century, when wooden handles began to be introduced, brushmakers mounted their brushes in quills. Quill brushes can still be had now. The size of the brush was determined, not by a number, but by the name of the bird which supplied each particular quill, lark, crow, duck, goose and swan – the largest, roughly equivalent to a modern number six.

The manufacture of the best brushes, like the making of hand-made paper, is labour-intensive, so they are not cheap; but a good brush, carefully treated, can last for years. They are made of animal hair from numerous sources; the best known are listed below. In the case of the best brushes, hair is taken only from the tip of the tail.
Red sable. The best, but by far the most expensive brushes, are pure red sable, made from the tail hairs of the kolinsky, an animal akin to the marten, found in Siberia. Reddish-yellow in colour, never exceeding 1½ in. (38 mm) in length, it is soft yet remarkably springy and comes to a fine point when dipped in water. A cheaper quality of red sable contains some ox hair taken from the ears of certain cattle.
Camelhair. Camelhair brushes are really made from a species of Siberian squirrel, although the best hair comes from Kazan. These are the softest type of brushes, varying in colour through red, blue, grey and black, and can be up to 3 in. (76 mm) in length.
Badger. Badger-hair brushes, used for fine finishing, are greyish in colour, with a black band about half an inch from the tip. This is the

only hair in brushmaking taken from the pelt rather than the tail.

Some other hairs used in making watercolour brushes are fitch, brownish black in colour, which comes from the skunk, dark grey Russian sable and black sable from the South American civet.

Much skill goes into the manufacture of the best watercolour brushes. First the hairs are carefully selected and graded, the longest ones in the centre with the shorter ones ranged about them, all facing in the same direction, and tied together in bunches. Each bunch is individually inserted, 'flag' end first (the flag end is the point that grows out of the animal), into a hollow, brass 'cannon' of the required size and shape. The cannon is tapped until the hairs settle well into it, then the root ends, the 'butts', are trimmed, tied and glued into the metal ferrule with thermoplastic cement. It is a time-consuming process and makes the best watercolour brushes, particularly the larger sizes, extremely expensive.

4
The Camera Obscura

Traditionally, nearly all watercolour artists began their pictures with a preliminary drawing in pencil, chalk, charcoal or ink, over which they glazed their tints or washes. Sometimes the drawing itself is dominant, with colour applied in subservient tints; at other times the lightly pencilled structure of the picture disappears beneath washes of powerful colour. Most of the great 18th-century painters in watercolour put great emphasis on careful preliminary drawing, whether it were a detailed study of the subject or a few deft but accurate touches in pencil to indicate the outlines of the composition. David Cox, despite the direct fluency of his watercolours, set great store by this, advising his pupils to study well the structural basis of their pictures: '. . . he who devotes his time to the completion of a perfect outline has more than half finished his piece.'

During the 18th century it was the practice of artists to add colour to a dominant drawing made with pen and ink and monochrome ink washes. A notable exception was Thomas Gainsborough, who anticipated future watercolourists by working his colour over a chalk drawing. In fact ink, particularly 'Indian' ink (really Chinese, but imported via India), was considered an important, if not the most important, part of a watercolour artist's equipment. Great interest was

Eighteenth-century engraving demonstrating how the image was projected in a camera obscura

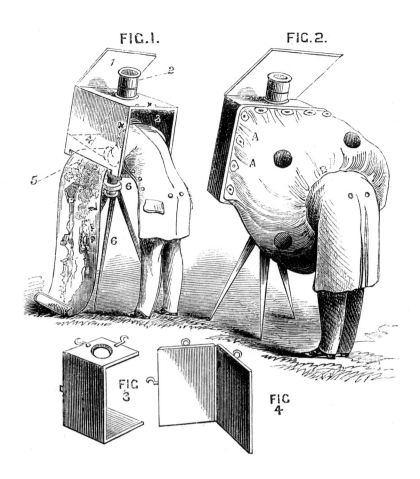

FIG.1. FIG.2.

FIG 3

FIG 4

Many eighteenth-century artists, particularly the topographical ones, made use of the camera obscura as an aid to accurate drawing

shown in producing black inks by a variety of methods, using at times the oddest ingredients to obtain a colour personally pleasing to the artist. Soot mixed with gum water, which had a rich, matt quality, was in common use during this period. More exotic blacks were prepared by grinding the black, burnt crust of a loaf, or blackened, parched split peas in gum water.

Many 18th-century artists made use of the camera obscura, the forerunner of the modern camera, as an aid in drawing. The camera obscura ('dark chamber') was probably invented by a 16th-century Neapolitan, Giovanni Battista della Porta, but it was during the 18th century that it really came into its own. Essentially it was a box open on one side over which a curtain was hung. A small double convex lens, fitted into a set of bellows to allow focussing, transmitted light to a mirror, which in turn projected the image being viewed directly on to sheet of ground glass or translucent paper on the base of the box. In the darkness of the box, his head shrouded by the curtain, the artist could trace at leisure the image of the landscape or building projected on the paper. (By the early years of the 19th century, pioneers such as Niepce and Daguerre were experimenting with methods to fix the image on sensitized paper – the beginnings of photography.)

This ingenious device, folding into a box no more twenty-five inches long and four inches deep, could be erected in a few minutes and saved the artist hours of painstaking observation and drawing. In a relatively short time he could trace his subject directly on to the paper, confident that the perspective and detail were totally accurate. Although it was a mechanical process and often resulted in a hard, insensitive outline, it could, in the hands of a master with a naturally sensitive line such as Paul Sandby, be used to produce true works of art.

5

Watercolour in the Caves

From about 35,000 BC Cro-Magnon man, the direct ancestor of modern man, began to inhabit the narrow valleys of the Dordogne, in the French foothills of the Pyrenees, and the mountainous region bordering the north coast of Spain. Here, in this world of limestone pock-marked with caves, he created magnificent paintings of the animals he hunted, masterpieces of observation drawn and painted with a remarkable degree of spirit and vitality.

Tools, animal bones and fire hearths excavated at successive levels show that he lived in shallow caves and overhangs facing across the valleys. Yet his animal paintings are found in deep subterranean caves, many of them in almost inaccessible niches and shafts. Only the most powerful urge, the urge to survive, could have driven ancient man to venture as far as twelve hundred metres into the mysterious, dark galleries and narrow winding passages.

The art of the hunter was not painted to be admired, for it was never seen. Rather, it was part of some sympathetic magic ritual, intended to ensure success in the chase. To these people the images of the animals they painted were real and they made them as lifelike as possible – a direct link with the live ones outside. When they depicted

In this detail of a frieze from Lascaux, aurochs (wild bulls) mingle with nervous deer and a herd of wild horses. The curious red-ochre marking above the muzzle of the auroch is believed to represent a symbolic trap

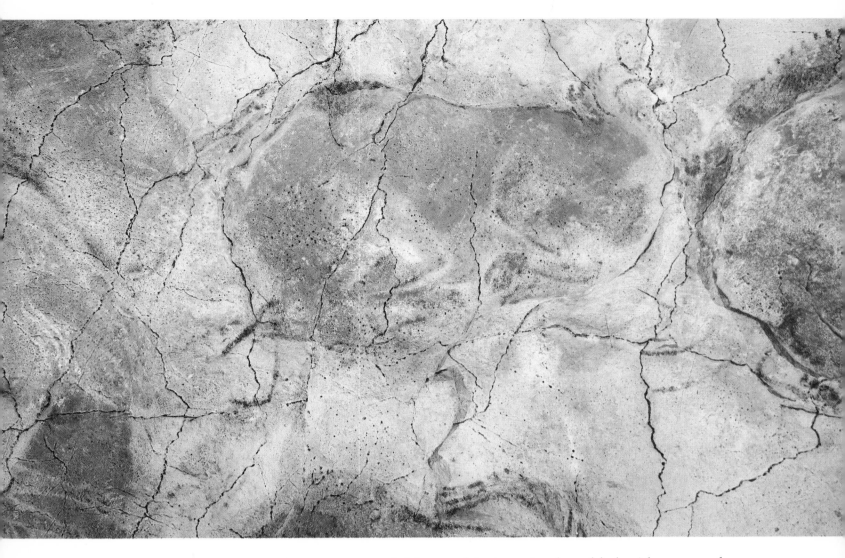

This dying bison from Altamira is a fine example of the realism that prehistoric artists brought to their paintings

a successful hunt with the animal studded with spears, they were hoping to bring about exactly that situation on their next hunting trip (there are communities in existence today that carry out similar rituals). The paintings were naturalistic in the strictest sense – closely adhering to nature – rather than realistic, capturing the attitude and expression of their quarry. Here, a herd of deer, painted in red ochre, dashes across the ceiling of a cave, there a mighty bison crouches in its last death agony; or a group of small, brown horses stands quietly, the mares heavy with foal. Often outlined in black, they show vigorous, true-to-life movement. The full magnitude of their achievement becomes apparent when we realize that the work was carried out by the feeble light of rushlight torches and crude, guttering lamps filled with animal fat.

Prehistoric artist hunters were limited to a simple palette, but their colours, particularly at Lascaux, remain dense and brilliant. Chemical analysis has shown the blacks to be made from manganese earths and bone charcoal. Colours ranging from yellow through the light reds to brown and crimson were made from earth pigments and mineral oxides; they had no blues or greens. The colours were ground to a fine powder and usually mixed with water, particularly when the colour was sprayed on, with great skill, through small blowpipes of hollow bone. These paintings – man's first watercolours – although their pigments were unbound, have been preserved by the chemical action of the limestone surface on which they were painted – a fortuitous process similar to the deliberate technique of fresco painting. Bone containers for the colours have been found near the sites of the paintings.

Early hunter artists are believed to have applied colour with their fingers, daubed it on with a stick and, as many of the paintings at Lascaux clearly show, painted it on with a brush, probably made from bunches of feathers or hair. Often the outlines and contours are accentuated by lines engraved with sticks, flints or antlers. Although there are forty known painted caves in south-west France and nearly as many in northern Spain, the accepted masterpieces are to be found at Altamira in Spain, Lascaux in the Dordogne and Niaux and Les Trois Frères in the French Pyreneean group of caves.

On the ceiling of the painted hall in the Altamira cavern animals of various species rub shoulders in a haphazard, crowded group; some of them are as much as two metres long. The individual treatment of each separate animal demonstrates amazing powers of observation and an ability to draw and paint from memory in a lively, skilful fashion. A wild boar 1.5 metres long, mainly painted in black, displays all the force and power of the real animal.

The animals in the Lascaux paintings, although not as accurately observed as those at Altamira, are technically more elaborate and represent a skilled attempt to produce polychromatic painting. The main hall at Lascaux is dominated by giant aurochs (wild bulls), over three metres long. The animals depicted in the frieze on the vault of the main hall, believed to have been painted by one artist, are meant to be seen together as a single composition. A strange creature, the 'Apocalyptic Beast', has crept into the herds of aurochs, horses and nervous deer. Believed by some to depict a unicorn, it is totally out of keeping with the other keenly observed animals. Its significance remains a mystery. The curious red-ochre markings above the muzzle of the one auroch are believed to represent a symbolic trap.

The cave and rock paintings of Cro-Magnon man, the Franco-Cantabrian hunter style, seem to leapfrog from northern Spain to the rock shelters of the Atlas mountains. To date there is no evidence to suggest a gradual movement south through the rest of Spain. From Algeria the influence can be traced through East Africa to the southern tip of the continent. Polychrome paintings of cattle made between 5000 and 1200 BC, discovered on the Tassili massif in Algeria, echo the style of the European hunters, a style that the Kalahari Bushmen in the south kept alive until the middle of the 19th century. Similar cave paintings appear in New Guinea and Australia, where the last example was produced as recently as the 1930s.

Overleaf: The horned goddess or 'White Lady' at Tassili in Algeria

A large composite rock painting from Mtoko Cave, Zimbabwe

6

Painting for Eternity

The cave art of the hunter gatherers was wholly practical in the sense that it was exclusively concerned with hunting wizardry. It made no attempt to decorate or delight; there was certainly no glimmering of 'art for art's sake'. Although of great vigour and – to our eyes – artistic value, it had little or no effect on the development of the visual arts of the Western world, which began in the agrarian empires of the Near East.

As nomadic hunter gatherers took to cultivating the soil and domesticating the animals they had previously hunted, settlements began to appear on the sunny, well-watered uplands at the edge of the Arabian, Syrian and Iranian deserts and along the banks of the Tigris, Euphrates and Nile. These agrarian communities built permanent dwellings, palaces for their rulers and sacred temples in which to worship. For magic was giving way to religion.

From the 6th millenium BC the Egyptians believed in life after death, and their art was directed by a compulsive need to recreate life – one Egyptian word for sculpture meant 'He-who-keeps-alive'. Pottery, ornaments, tools and food were placed in the grave and the corpse laid on its side facing west. As the burial grounds were always to the east of the village, this allowed the dead to watch over the living. By about 3000 BC the whole of Egypt was ruled by the

Fowling in the Marshes, a beautifully observed wall painting from the tomb of Nebamun at Thebes, dating back to 1400 BC (British Museum, London)

pharaohs, god kings with absolute power. The pharaoh was the father of his people, and the whole country was devoted to his interests. When he died he became a god in the Underworld and his son succeeded him, becoming a god on earth.

The Egyptians believed that the after life of the soul depended on the preservation of the body, so the corpses of pharaohs, nobles and high officials were mummified before being placed in the burial chamber. During the earlier dynasties, on the death of an important man it was the grim custom to sacrifice his servants and slaves to assure that he was adequately served in the nether world. Later, this fearful practice was replaced by substituting painted images of servants. Often, painted friezes depicting events in the life of the dead man adorned the walls, accompanied by hieroglyphic texts: writing and painting were closely related in Egypt, the hierogylphic signs themselves being conventionalized pictures. As in the case of primitive cave art, Egyptian tomb painting was not created to be publicly seen and admired; only the soul of the dead man would ever gaze upon the beautifully depicted scenes.

Egyptians were not allowed to develop as independent individuals, and even their art was anonymous.

The painting itself was almost diagrammatic, the artists subject to a rigid set of rules and conventions from which they dared not deviate. Although at first glance difficult to understand, Egyptian art is completely logical. Much in the manner of a child's approach to painting, though infinitely more rational, the Egyptian artist constructed his pictures and forms to give maximum visual information. The picture was two-dimensional: very little attempt was made to create illusionist space as in Western art; the result was more a map than a picture as we know it. Perspective was unknown, and

Inspection of Geese. This wall painting, also from the tomb of Nebamun at Thebes, is a good example of the logical approach of the Egyptian artist, though the figure on the extreme left has its shoulder turned completely sideways (British Museum, London)

scale was determined by the size and importance of individual elements within the picture. The pharaoh towers above his wife and children, who have their arms around his calves; his enemies in battle scenes are depicted as tiny figures easily crushed; sometimes bearers of offerings lead in minute animals.

Each form within a picture is drawn from its most characteristic angle. The features of the head are best seen in profile, but the eye from the front; thus it seemed perfectly logical to the Egyptian artist to place a full-face eye on the side view of a face. It also appeared sensible to him to depict the shoulders and chest from the front (to show how the arms joined the body) while drawing the legs from the side (to show how they moved). The inside view of the foot was usually adopted, with the big toe nearest the viewer; this gave the figure either two right or two left feet.

The Egyptian artist showed things as they should be, not as they actually were. This idealization applied in particular to the major figures within a composition; they appear in the full bloom of life, the men strong and well made, the women small-breasted, young and slim. In many of the Old Kingdom tomb paintings, less important characters are old and balding; often they quarrel, fight, run and hunt, while the principal figures are normally tranquil and serene.

The artists – it is believed that they worked as a group, each member of which had his own expertise – first levelled the stone surface with a layer of clay, which was brushed over with a fine gypsum plaster wash. It was then squared up into a grid which ensured an accurate representation of the scene to be painted. Up to the twenty-sixth dynasty, the grid of the human figure – each important figure was gridded separately – was based on squares the size of the human fist; the distance from the base line to the hairline of the figure being eighteen squares. The carefully executed initial drawing served as a basis for painting.

Their brushes were probably reed stems, chewed and splayed out at the ends, and palm fibre, but judging by the fineness of much of

Weighing of the heart of the scribe Ani, from the *Book of the Dead,* painted on papyrus (British Museum, London)

25

the work, these must have been cunningly shaped, coming to a fine point. A subtle range of colour was squeezed from a limited palette – blacks made from charcoal and soot, white lime, yellow and red ochres, greens and blues derived from malachite, azurite and powdered enamels. These water-based pigments were mixed together or thinned out to achieve an extraordinarily varied range of colour. Ochres were used to paint the bodies of human beings and animals (men were usually darker than women). Black was used for hair, white for clothes, blue and green for background decoration and foliage. Many earthenware bowls and shells, used as water pots and pigment containers, have been found near unfinished paintings, some with powdered colour still in them.

Paper, made from the pith of the papyrus plant, was used by the priests and scribes to record religious and historical events. Thanks to the hot, dry clin.ate of Egypt, these scroll paintings are still remarkably well preserved, their colours bright and fresh. The papyrus scrolls comprising *The Book of the Dead* are one of the earliest examples of the use of a strip-cartoon technique to tell a story. It is difficult to believe that these watercolours, glowing with colour and lovingly executed, were painted purely as a record without any conscious effort to create beauty.

Opposite: The Sacred Herd of Heaven, *Book of the Dead,* 1250 BC (British Museum, London)

Below: A banqueting scene with musicians in the foreground, a typical example of a strip-cartoon technique (British Museum, London)

7

Classical Painting

Opposite: Despite their preoccupation with death, the Etruscans depicted a sense of pleasure and joy in their frescoes. This flute player from the tomb of Triclinio at Tarquinia is full of life and movement

Below: Bull-jumping from a Minoan frieze. The artists revelled in the use of spontaneous colour for its own sake, rather than reproducing natural colour (Heraklion Museum)

At some time before 4000 BC Stone Age farmers – possibly from the Near East, Anatolia, Mesopotamia or even Egypt – settled on the island of Crete, which became a natural stepping stone between the eastern Mediterranean countries, Egypt and the mainland of Europe. The climate was ideal for farming, with warm summers, mild winters and a good rainfall. The Minoans grew wheat, herded sheep and cattle and fished, drawing much of the subject matter for their frescoes from these activities. The island rapidly became an important trading centre; merchants and traders came from every part of the known world, bringing with them new ideas, which were woven into the unique Minoan culture. Although in the beginning influenced by Egypt and Mesopotamia – Crete may have been colonized by the Egyptians around 3500 BC – the culture of Crete was fundamentally different from those of the great agrarian empires. Far from the austere, rigid society of Egypt, dominated by a god-like pharaoh and an all-powerful priesthood, it concerned itself with nature and living people enjoying life.

This reveals itself most clearly in the paintings, those vigorous, boldly coloured wall paintings which decorate the palaces and temples. The formal art of Egypt gave way to an art full of lively colour and movement; the artist, delighting in his natural surroundings, in turn delighted the viewer. European art had been born.

The Minoan artists revelled in the use of spontaneous colour for its

A banqueting scene from the Etruscan Tomb of the Leopards, Tarquinia

own sake, rather than reproducing the true natural colours. This was nature in terms of decoration. Blue monkeys frolic in a countryside of vivid reds and blues, pale pinks and greens. Electric-blue dolphins with a bright yellow streak down their sides swim through a pale straw sea; the 'Prince of the Lilies' – probably a priest king – wearing a crown of lilies and peacock plumes on his flowing black hair, stands pale pink against a bright red ground. But the most common motif is the octopus. Writhing around elegantly formed pots, it is the product of astonishing observation and 'feel' for the movement of the creature.

A severe earthquake destroyed the first phase of Minoan civilization, but the islanders had already begun to colonize the cities of Mycenae and Tiryns on the Greek mainland, and it was from these cities that the impetus came to rebuild Knossos. Under King Minos, Crete dominated the Aegean, receiving tribute (often human) from other settlements in the area. But by 1400 BC Mycenae had replaced Crete as the leader in the Aegean. Invaders sweeping down from the north destroyed the cities of the Aegean and their commerce, bringing to a sudden end a thousand years of civilization. Three hundred years of comparative darkness followed, until the civilization of Classical Greece finally emerged.

Greek art and culture reached a peak during the 5th century BC – the Classical golden age. Passionately devoted to man the individual, the Greeks glorified the ideal human figure in both painting and sculpture. They saw their gods as perfectly proportioned men and women; not for them the animal-headed gods of Mesopotamia and the Nile. Sophocles said, 'Wonders are many, and nothing is more wonderful than man'.

Tragically, all that remains of Greek painting is a few fragments of fresco, the painted scenes on pottery and some contemporary descriptions. However, the influence of the painters spread to colonies and cities established outside Greece, where the style as well as many of the actual wall paintings were copied. It is from these frescoes and mosaics that we obtain a glimpse of the painting of the Greek cities.

The Hellenistic style of the fourth century made art more dynamic, introducing a greater degree of emotion. Crowded with realistic and dramatic detail, a mosaic of Alexander's victory over Darius, copied from a famous contemporary work, can still be seen today in the museum at Naples. In this action-packed mosaic the three-quarter-view figures display movement and vitality. Gone are the flat, side-on views of the Egyptian frescoes: illusionist space had begun to appear in Western art.

Greek art had a special influence on a people living in central Italy, the Etruscans. Little is known of their antecedents, but they obviously had a passion for painting and followed Greek examples in their frescoes. The Etruscans had an obsessive concern for the dead; to them the tomb was the dwelling place of the souls of the dead in the hereafter. With great care they fashioned these tombs to resemble their own house interiors, providing the dead with all the comforts of home – couches on which to recline, ceiling beams and door frames, all cut in stone. The walls they decorated with fresco paintings of funeral wakes and scenes of earthly pleasures. By 400 BC, these tombs had grown into vast tumuli, with enough rooms to house a family of up to thirty people.

Despite the Etruscans' concern with death, their wall paintings depict a sense of pleasure and joy of living, as well as showing keen

Left: A sensitively painted figure depicting Spring, from a Roman fresco (National Museum, Naples)

Overleaf: *Love Feast of Silenus* (Villa of the Mysteries, Pompeii)

31

observation and love of narrative. As a man dives from a rock, straight as an arrow, into the sea, his companions watch him from a boat, oars rested; a dolphin leaps from the water and a flight of birds soars upwards. In another frieze a man and girl perform an energetic ritual dance to the music of a double flute. In the early wall paintings the rock was smoothed flat and the pigments, mixed with water and an adhesive binder, were applied directly to the surface. Generally the artist painted on fresh, moist plaster, a technique calling for immediate decision, speed and a sure touch. Later, a method of painting on dry plaster was devised. At times a few subtly contrasting, light-toned colours were used; at other times the colour was rich and brilliant.

Overrun by Celts from the north and the Romans from the south, Etruscan civilization dwindled and died; but not before it had influenced its great enemy with its art, culture and religion. The Romans drew on both Etruscan and Hellenistic art to evolve a style in which secular subjects began to take precedence over religious ones. Our knowledge of the Classical painting of the Mediterranean stems mainly from the extensive Roman wall paintings which can be seen in much the same condition as when they were first painted due, ironically enough, to the eruption of Vesuvius in AD 79, which buried Pompeii, Herculaneum and Stabiae and preserved many of the murals intact. Virtually every building, however humble, had some form of decoration, either mosaic or painted in water-bound colours. From 175 to 80 BC the colour is usually soft and applied with great skill, in sensitive brush strokes, against a red or dark green background. This gave way to an Architectural style, in which the artists sought to extend their paintings beyond the walls to create a sense of space, using columns, doors and windows to achieve a three-dimensional effect. In the Ornate style, AD 1 to 50, the wall is divided into a series of pictures, usually framed by slender, twisted columns. From AD 50 to the eruption of Vesuvius, the style is described as Intricate. The complex frescoes are reminiscent of Baroque painting.

Most of the paintings of Pompeii are not true frescoes (painted directly on moist lime plaster). The artists used a stucco lustre method, in which a pigment of marble dust is mixed with wet plaster and painted on in layers. A mixture of soap and potash was used as a binding agent.

Meanwhile, in other parts of the world, painting was moving in entirely different directions. In the Far East Chinese artists were forming their own approach towards watercolour painting.

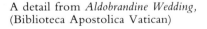

A detail from *Aldobrandine Wedding*, (Biblioteca Apostolica Vatican)

8

Watercolour Painting in the Far East

Throughout the history of painting it is only in the Far East that the use of pure watercolour was developed as the exclusive means of visual expression.

To appreciate Oriental painting, it is essential to put aside the preconceived ideas of the West, and see the wall paintings, horizontal scrolls and paper screens of China and Japan as extensions of poetry and calligraphy. In the Far East paintings were produced for an elite audience, sometimes for the sole enjoyment of the artist himself; they were poetical arrangements of nature, to be appreciated only by the initiated. The Oriental artist has never been fettered by the fads of a patron or the dictates of a dominant Church; he has never felt himself obliged to attempt social reform by satirical comment. Nor has he been called upon to depict nature as faithfully as possible; rather, he has been encouraged to look upon painting as a means of conveying an emotion. Perhaps no other school of painting has ever made such demands on the viewer, who is required to understand subtle illusions and quotations, to capture the fine nuances of mood, as well as to appreciate the bold precision of brushwork.

The Chinese view of life evolved in different ways from that of the Middle East or the West and was naturally closely connected with the direction in which their visual arts developed. To them, man was not the greatest achievement of creation, made by God in His own likeness; on the contrary, he was regarded very much as an afterthought. Beside the beauties of nature – the mountains and valleys, trees and flowers – he counted for very little, though he did strive to contemplate and understand the wonders which surrounded him. Confucius maintained that since the supernatural is beyond man's

Birds and Flowers. This detail of a hand scroll painted in ink and colours on silk shows the sureness of line that was developed in 'boneless' paintings. Chao Chi (Hui Tsung, Chinese Emperor, reigned 1101-1126) (British Library, London)

叁 西汉帛画局部之二

comprehension, he should not waste time worrying about it, but should concentrate on discovering the best way of living on this earth. The humility of the Oriental in the face of the grandeur of nature is summed up by the Taoist philosopher, Chuan Tze, 'The life of man passes like a galloping horse, changing at every turn, at every hour. What ought he to do, or what ought he not to do, except allow his own decomposition to continue?' This attitude persisted, and whereas early Western civilization was in a perpetual state of development, the cultures of the Far East carried on with little obvious change until quite recent times.

The culture of China did not flourish in total isolation. Influences and ideas flowed both east and west along the silk routes, the caravan routes which linked Europe with central Asia and China. Yet, during the period of the Han dynasty (206 BC to AD 220) Chinese cultural attitudes crystallized, laying the foundations of a definitive art which was to spread into Korea and Japan.

It was natural that watercolour should develop along the lines it did in the Far East, for at an early age youngsters were given a pointed brush with which to write. The manual dexterity that came with the use of this brush in the precise delineation of calligraphic forms was also employed to interpret the surroundings in painting. With no compulsion to reproduce and illustrate nature faithfully, the Oriental painter saw little reason for perspective, chiaroscuro or realistic modelling. It was enough to capture the essence of life around him.

In China the most admired painters were scholars. They were intellectuals who had passed the imperial examinations to become civil servants, the highest category to which an individual could aspire – the nobility in effect. They painted for mutual enjoyment, probing the depths of their own experience and knowledge and displaying it for the enjoyment of those able to understand it. Paradoxically, the fact that this art was highly formalized (in Japan there were seventy-two important laws governing painting) in no way inhibited the painter from expressing an overwhelming, totally subjective sense of beauty. The viewer was invited to enter the painting, to be surrounded by mysterious misty valleys, to feel the excitement of bursting buds, to experience the overpowering sense of depth and scale.

Opposite: Han Dynasty painting of 200 BC – AD 220, *Legend of the Nine Sons*. This detail, painted in ink and colours on silk, comes from a tomb at Ma-wang-tui, Ch'ang-sha, Hunan Province (British Museum, London)

Below: Kun Ts'An. *A Chinese Winter Landscape,* dated 1666 (British Museum, London)

Spontaneity was achieved by the 'strength of the brush stroke' – in Japan the law of *fude no chikara*. As the point of the brush touched the surface of silk or paper, the artist strove to communicate an inner feeling, which flowed through his arm and hand to the tip of his brush and so into the content of his painting. By first achieving peace of mind, the artist arrived at a calm sympathy with the world of nature. This was the only way to achieve harmony with nature; by the absolute co-ordination of mind and hand he could identify himself with it.

The words of one Chinese scholar painter, Wên T'ung, who specialized in painting bamboo, puts in a nutshell the Oriental approach to painting. 'When you are going to paint a bamboo, you must first realize the thing completely in your mind. Then grasp the brush, fix your attention so that you can see clearly what you wish to paint. Start quickly, move the brush, follow straight what you see before you, as the buzzard swoops when the hare jumps out. If you hesitate one moment, it is gone.'

Chinese and Japanese artists worked either on paper or silk; both surfaces were slightly absorbent and once a brush stroke had been made it could not be obliterated. In Far Eastern painting the brush itself was all important. Whereas in Western watercolours, particularly landscape and flower painting, the viewer takes time looking for evidence of faithful observation on the part of the artist, in Oriental painting there is an immediate impression of life, growth and movement. This is chiefly due to the sureness of the ink line and the crisp drawing of the colour in 'boneless' paintings (those without a constricting outline) which was obtained by using soft but springy brushes, made from the tail hair of fox, hare and sable and coming naturally to a single point. Held in bamboo handles, the brushes ranged from fine to large and thick-bodied, but all came to a sharp point above the swelling of the body.

Solid cakes and sticks of ink were diluted with water to create the required tones, which ranged from opulent black to the palest of soft greys. The colour pigments, slightly stiffened with gum, were ground from mineral colours, and used at much the same, light consistency as the ink. These pigments could not be mixed in the same manner as Western water-based colours to produce an infinite range of shades. The colour strength was controlled by mixing the pigment with shell white, obtained from ground seashells. This was used in both China

Opposite: Kano Motonobu, sixteenth century *Pheasants and Peonies*. (Kyoto Museum, Japan)

Below: *The Five Holy Mountains*. The viewer is invited to enter the painting, to be surrounded by mysterious misty valleys, towering crags and formalized trees (National Palace Museum of Taiwan)

Tosa School, c.1800. One of a series of drawings in ink, body colour and gold illustrating the life and pastimes of the Japanese Court (Victoria and Albert Museum, London)

and Japan as a base over which to float clear, bright pigments.

In their technique and brush control, the scholar painters reached breathtaking perfection; with a single deft stroke, they produced a leaf, a petal, a whole cluster of bamboo. Often a light-and-shade effect was achieved by washing on a second colour while the first was still wet. Although the colours ran together, they did not actually mix; each remained clearly visible. The more highly skilled painters – the Japanese Maruyama-Shijō masters in particular – sometimes charged a wide brush with different tones of the same colour, which enabled them to give the impression of modelling with a single sweep of the brush.

Many European artists later obtained extraordinary tone, scale, even implied colour, with simple monochrome techniques – but this was never looked upon as an art form in its own right. Only the painters in ink of China and Japan took a single colour, black, and used it to create complexities of light and shade, tone and scale, life and movement. This practice stemmed directly from brush-drawn calligraphy, an art form more highly prized even than painting. The need to keep each character the same height, to position it accurately and where necessary – with a deft flick of the brush – tail it off to a sharp point, provided the discipline required to execute an ink painting. Because 'colour is an illusion, and illusion is colour', it was abandoned. It inhibited intuition.

Ink paintings were carried out at tremendous speed. Great care was taken to obtain a rich, velvety, black ink, one that could be diluted with water to give an infinite range of dove-grey shades. Usually made from the soot of burnt pinewood, it was mixed with animal glue and moulded into cakes or sticks (it was to become known as Indian ink in the West). This was rubbed down on an inkstone, a flat slab of stone sloping into a well, where it was diluted to the required shade.

9
Islamic and Indian Miniatures

With the words of the Prophet ringing in their ears, the followers of Muhammad conquered the greater part of the known world in the 7th and 8th centuries – a region half as large again as the Roman empire. They reached the frontiers of China in 732 and occupied northern India. In the west they spread across North Africa and conquered most of Spain, penetrating deep into France.

Unlike some earlier conquerors, they did not destroy cities and

Mughal period. *Akbar crossing the Ganges*, 1567. In this painting one artist, Ikhlas, drew the outline and painted it while another, Madhu, was responsible for the portraits (Victoria and Albert Museum, London)

enslave their inhabitants. Anyone prepared to turn to Islam was accepted as an equal, and local customs and traditions were respected. While they introduced a new way of life and a new political system, they had little in the way of a native aesthetic tradition and no urban culture. Islamic art therefore evolved from the art of the conquered

Rejoicing on the birth of Salim, later Emperor Jahangir, c.1590. The outline was drawn by Kesu Kalan, the painting executed by Dharmadas (Victoria and Albert Museum, London)

peoples, an art revitalized, certainly, stimulated to a new creative awareness, and in time unified in a single, vigorous style.

Christian art was characterized by great diversity between different periods and countries. From the Renaissance at least, Christian artists sought the original and the unfamiliar, exploring problems of perspective, spatial relationships and chiaroscuro. In Islamic art there

was a higher degree of uniformity. Inevitably, each region within the vast world of Islam had its own characteristics and national tendencies, but in general Islamic art followed patterns hallowed by time and convention.

While the religious leaders of Islam dictated the design of religious architecture, it was the pleasure-loving caliphs, following the example of Christian Byzantium, who created and encouraged the graphic arts. These were dedicated to the glory of these princes, who, from the first Umayyad caliph onwards, invited (or compelled) artists from east and west to come to work in their capital at Damascus. At an early stage in the development of Islamic art, Syrian, Egyptian and Persian artists interpreted the styles of their own and other parts of Islam, adopting them to conform with Muslim beliefs. At the same time a calligraphic script of great beauty was universally accepted throughout Islam, from India to Spain. Treated as decoration, it became an integral part of Islamic painting.

Strict Muslim doctrine forbade the making of images, the representation of any living creature, human or animal. There is no reference to this in the Koran, but in the *Traditions of the Prophet*, Muhammad is quoted as having said that painters would undergo cruel, infernal punishment for having the temerity to imitate the creative acts of the Almighty. This doctrine was enforced by religious leaders who succeeded in eliminating the decorative use of images in the mosques, but it had hardly any effect on secular art; the hedonist caliphs continued to commission wall paintings, illustrated books and picture albums.

Fresco painting was never neglected by the Islamic artists, but it is the miniature that most aptly expresses the beauty of Islamic art. The artists painted almost entirely for the caliph and his court, the royal patrons commissioning illustrated books and exquisitely detailed picture albums. The restrictive format of these rather small books governed both style and content; there is a wealth of closely observed detail, depicted superbly in rich, intense colour. Brilliantly drawn calligraphic script is a vital part of the design. These miniatures are generally full of incident, of bustling, active figures, though later the single figure became more important: a young girl standing perfectly still on a terrace holding a single lotus blossom; or a man sleeping beneath an idealized willow tree.

The usual medium was gouache, the powdered pigments being mixed with egg or gum, and although the artists were denied the subtle nuances of European watercolour and Chinese inks, they handled their extensive range of colour in a unique and satisfying manner. The technique obviously discouraged the use of line, yet each unit within the picture was delineated with great precision. These paintings were executed on highly prepared paper of a quality that has withstood the wear of many centuries.

The types of books illustrated ranged from medical treatises to herbals, bestiaries, lyrical and epic poetry and historical sagas. In one, a Persian prince shoots a white water bird with his bow as it flies above a fast-flowing, azure river; in another, an early 13th-century translation of a Greek treatise on medicine, a man shouts as he is bitten by an angry, elongated dog, with red, lolling tongue. The subject matter is vast and varied and, although to the Western eye accustomed to an infinite variety of styles it may appear to have a degree of sameness, closer familiarity dispels this impression.

Islamic art benefited from Chinese, Indian, Mongolian and other traditions, and in turn exerted a reciprocating influence on them.

Hindu art was losing its impetus, stagnating in lifeless convention, when northern and central India were overrun by Muslim armies at the turn of the 13th century. The clashing of two distinct cultures resulted in a revitalization of Hindu civilization. The vivid colour of Muslim painting did much to strengthen the naturally delicate and subdued colour of Hindu art, though without destroying its individuality. It also gave a unity to the content of Hindu painting.

In the 16th century India was conquered by the Mughals. During the hundred years covered by the reigns of Akbar, Jahangir and Shah Jahan (1555–1658) the Mughal style of Muslim India was developed, far surpassing any previous achievement in Muslim India. In painting especially, a new standard of excellence was set and one of the finest schools of Islamic painting created. The greatest of the early works of this school was the *Dastan-i Amir Hamza*, the largest known Muslim manuscript illustrated with full-page paintings (only a few of which, unfortunately, survive). Though early Mughal painting was strongly influenced by Persia, the Hindu tradition was by no means submerged. Some of the most impressive works are small manuscripts of great delicacy on fine, polished paper, the margins minutely decorated with exquisite gold landscapes, animals and flowers that match the quality of the graceful calligraphy. Historical narrative painting, often celebrating the lives of the emperors, arose later in the period, and portrait painting reached the highest standard. Realism became a powerful force in Mughal painting, especially in scenes of everyday life and in the many beautiful animal paintings of the reign of Shah Jahan.

Radha and Krishna walking in a Grove. Kangrac, 1820-25 (Victoria and Albert Museum, London)

10

To the Glory of God

From its humble and obscure beginning in Palestine, Christianity spread quickly through the Roman empire. Its message of love and hope, eagerly accepted by rich and poor alike, marked the end of the ancient Classical world, whose logical aestheticism had been based on realism and physical beauty. Greek and Roman thought, born on the principle of unity and harmony as manifested in the human body, at first rebelled against Christianity. Its Eastern influences carried the seed of dualism: the universe was seen to be divided into two irreconcilable powers: good and evil, light and darkness, the spirit and the flesh. Man was urged to soar to spiritual heights beyond reason and logic.

Fearful of persecution, the early Christians met secretly in the catacombs on the outskirts of Rome, and soon these underground cemeteries became strongholds of the rapidly expanding religion. Here, in an endless maze of passages dotted with tombs or *loculi* cut into the walls, they began to establish a Christian art. By the feeble light of oil lamps, under constant fear and stress, they evolved the symbols of their new creed. The Virgin and Child, the Good Shepherd carrying the wayward lamb, the Peacock, symbol of eternal life (because its flesh was believed to be incorruptible), and the Fish, the most sacred of Christian symbols.

From the first, Christian painting expressed a fundamental belief in the life hereafter to which the believer should aspire. It was a hidden art, as Egyptian art had been, but unlike Egyptian painting, the Christian frescoes were painted to be seen by all who believed. The Christian artists based their style on existing pagan artistic tradition, deriving their forms from the contemporary art around them. They used a limited range of water-based colours, mainly reds, greens and yellow ochres. At first crude and hurriedly executed, their work gradually gained in artistic merit. When Christianity became an official religion, the painters were able to decorate the countless churches that sprang up throughout the Roman empire. Christianity prospered, but Rome fell. The Emperor Constantine, who had officially recognized Christianity, built a new city, Constantinople, in the east. In the west, Germanic tribes overran the empire, taking Rome herself in 401.

During the ensuing centuries the centres of learning and culture moved to the monasteries of Ireland and Northumbria. From the *scriptoria* of these monasteries came the beautiful illuminated manuscripts which, although small in scale, became the basis for Western art. These monastic workshops worked in an ornate, native style, giving new and unexpected impetus to the old, pre-Christian, Celtic spirit, whose ornamentation was absorbed into Christian imagery.

One of the earliest monasteries was founded at Durrow in central Ireland by St Columba – 'the Dove' – around 553. Here the artist monks, working in watercolour on vellum, produced the first of the great manuscripts. Dating from the latter half of the seventh century, the *Book of Durrow*, a missal, incorporated Celtic spirals, curves and twists in its dynamic, brilliantly coloured, abstract patterns. Elaborately decorated capital letters encroach into margins before

Overleaf right: The title page of the *Book of Kells* which was started on Iona, Colum Cille – the 'cell of the Dove's Isle – and finished at Kells in Ireland (Trinity College, Dublin)

Overleaf left: Dating from the latter half of the seventh century, the *Book of Durrow* was the first of the great manuscripts (Trinity College Dublin)

hoenrano

spreading themselves across the page; here and there an animal head with gaping jaws peeps from among whorls and arabesques.

One manuscript followed another in a fervour of religious zeal; the *Lindisfarne Gospels*, the *Lichfield Gospels* and the *Book of Kells*; all were executed with an intensity of feeling for their subject that is hardly conceivable today. In these manuscripts, Celtic, Coptic, Anglo-Saxon and Scandinavian decorative elements were interwoven in a complex maze that appears to have no beginning and no end.

The elements of the book ornament used by the Celtic scribes were derived from textile techniques, plaiting and handweaving, which were later transferred to metalwork. Letter terminals of mythical and allegorical beasts (thought to represent demons, like Gothic gargoyles), animals, birds, snakes and lizards, combine with sinuous linear designs. The dog and dragon, the latter both winged and wingless according to the design requirements, is an ever-recurring motif in early illumination. Doves, fishes and lambs also appear in the manuscripts, but these creatures are never distorted, for they were sacred symbols: in legend the Devil could take the shape of any bird or beast except those. Such an art was not aimed at the secular public, but rather at the monks themselves and novices entering the priesthood.

As far as we know, the word 'illuminator', one who 'lighted up', originated in the 12th century. Allied to the art of heraldry, illuminated book decoration called for the use of bright colours and burnished gold. The skins of numerous animals, even fishes, have been used at times, but the monastic illuminator worked on vellum or parchment. Virgin parchment, or *aignellinus*, was made from the skins

Right: The Temptation from the *Book of Kells* (Trinity College, Dublin)

Opposite: The elaborate portrayal of the Four Evangelists from the *Book of Kells*. Realism has given way to abstract patterns of arabesque and curve (Trinity College, Dublin)

50

of stillborn lambs; ordinary parchment from that of fully grown sheep. Vellum was produced from calfskin, the thinnest and finest 'uterine vellum', being made from a stillborn calf. Some monasteries, such as the Abbey of Cluny in France, became celebrated for the careful preparation and fine quality of their *parcheminerie*. Illumination, growing out of the decoration of initial letters, came to acquire a pictorial content, illustrating a particular written passage.

With the *Book of Kells*, this style of illumination reached its most flamboyant phase: a frenzy of movement and decoration. St Columba withdrew from Ireland in 563 to found a religious community on the island of Iona which, through the missionary zeal of himself and his followers, became the centre of Christian civilization in northern Britain for the next two hundred and fifty years. It became known as Colum Cille – 'the cell of the Dove's Isle'. About 815, the Norse invasion of Iona drove the Columban community back to Ireland, to seek refuge in the monastery at Kells, twenty miles from Dublin, where they erected a new town of Colum Cille. Tradition has it that the *Book of Kells* – 'the Great Gospel of Colum Cille' was begun on Iona and carried by the then abbot Cellach and his fleeing community to be finished at Kells.

It contains the four New Testament Gospels of St Matthew, St Mark, St Luke and St John. Written in Latin on thick-glazed vellum, it measures 13½ in. × 9½ in. (332 × 227 mm) though it was probably 15 in. × 11 in. before being cut. The ink used in the script is brownish-black, but here and there the Irish minuscule hand is written in bluish-black, red or purple. It was originally designed for use during High Mass. Its cover, richly decorated with gold and precious stones, disappeared in 1006.

According to the *Annals of Ulster*, 'the Great Gospel of Colum Cille was stolen at night from the western Erdomh [sacristy] of the great Church of Ceannanus. This was the principal relic of the Western world on account of its singular cover: and it was found after twenty days and two months, its gold having been stolen off it, and a sod over it'.

The Celtic illuminator remorselessly translated into ornament any image he employed. The human figure was subjected to the same rules as abstract patterns: hair and beard became stylized coils; eyes, nose and mouth, calligraphic flourishes. The same calligraphic treatment was accorded to limbs and drapery, reducing them to the simplicity of stained-glass windows. Realism gave way to abstract patterns of arabesque and curve; the folds in fabric were picked out in a strongly contrasting colour. Hardly ever naturalistic, colour was applied in flat, even washes that filled patterned compartments with blue, purple, red, green and yellow; the face, hands and feet always remained white. Nowhere is the colour more wayward, the treatment more ornamental, than the colouring of the symbolic beasts of the Gospels that appear in 'The Evangelical Symbols'.

There was no light and shade in Celtic art, no attempt at modelling; every detail, clear and separate, was meticulously delineated; this can only be fully appreciated by examination under a magnifying glass. The blues and reds, mineral colours, were rich and opaque; the rest were thin and transparent. To obtain a greater brilliance of colour, some illuminators worked in egg tempera, a medium dating back to the 5th century. In this method the ground pigment was mixed with the yolk of egg, which bound the colour, allowing it to adhere to the surface of the vellum. Although water was the medium used to dilute the egg tempera while it was being worked, once it dried it became rock-hard and quite waterproof.

Sometimes a single scribe carried out a complete book by himself. First selecting and preparing the vellum, he would rule in guide lines with a fine metal point, copy the text, paint in the illumination, rub down the gold leaf, then bind and tool the cover. Generally, however, there was a division of labour among the members of the *scriptorium*, each man having his particular skill. One would scrape and polish the

Moses and the Egyptian, from the *Winchester Bible,* written and illuminated by the monks of St Swithin's, *c.*1160-1170 (Cathedral Library, Winchester)

vellum; another rule it and write the text; a third put in the initials, lay the gold and decorate the borders; a fourth would paint in the miniatures. In the case of the *Book of Kells*, it has been suggested that up to four monks were responsible for the illumination alone. There was a portraitist, an illustrator who painted the scenes from the life of Jesus, an artist who executed the highly decorative work and a fourth who devised the initials incorporating natural forms and demons.

One of the most ornately decorated medieval manuscripts, *The Golden Gospels of Echternach*, was written and illuminated in Luxembourg about 990. As many as ten different styles can be traced in the Gospels, which are sumptuous with gold; the cover is studded with precious gems. The script, a spiritual activity that represents the real value of sacred books, would have been written by a scholar, a cleric; it is believed that the rest of the work was carried out by laymen. These specialized craftsmen, working in large *scriptoria* or illuminators' workshops, prepared the materials, painted the illumination under the direction of the clerics and put the work together in the form of a book.

The 12th century saw an intellectual and artistic revolution that was to have a profound effect on Western thinking. The concept of Plato, preached by St Augustine, that ideals are more important than the physical world, that truth lay in the mind rather than the senses, began to give way to the teaching of Aristotle. In the words of Roger Bacon, 'there are two modes of knowledge, reason and experience [personal experiment]. No reason can give us certainty, the latter depends entirely on experiment.' Universities were founded at Salerno, Paris and Oxford. Chivalric romances were coming into vogue. It was the age into which St Francis of Assisi was born.

During this age of inquiry the *Winchester Bible* was begun. This large bible, now bound in three volumes, is the work of many scribes and illuminators who were engaged on it over a long period. It shows not only the development of artistic style in the 12th century, but the changing attitude towards observation. Originally written by the monks of St Swithins, Winchester, to be read during meals, it was reluctantly given by them to St Hugh, prior of Witham, at the firm request of King Henry II.

Unlike the *Book of Kells* and the Echternach *Gospels*, the figures in the illuminations of the *Winchester Bible* are modelled, and the modelling becomes more realistic as the work progresses. In the earlier work, the painting of the 'Master of the Leaping Figures' (the names of the artists who worked on the Bible at different times stem from a modern study by Walter Oakeshott) has dramatic curves and strong diagonals which give the impression of vehement movement. The figures themselves are modelled, but the modelling is treated as part of the design. The last set of illuminations in the *Winchester Bible*, those of the 'Master of Gothic Majesty', clearly show the move away from the earlier, Romanesque treatment. Here there is a greater sense of realism; the figures are carefully shaded, the gestures more natural; the subject matter is quieter, more restrained.

The need for illuminated manuscripts, patiently written and illuminated by monastic scholars to the greater glory of God, was curtailed by the introduction of printing. Guttenberg's invention of moveable type revolutionized the dissemination of information, incidentally loosening the hold of the Church by placing books within reach of a far wider public. The art of the illuminated book continued, but mainly as an art form, no longer as a primary means of communication. However, the work of the medieval illuminators was to have marked influence on the 'painters in little' who emerged in the 15th century.

11

Medieval Frescoes

When the monks and friars began to leave the monasteries to carry the Gospel to the people, they brought about a profound change in Western art. The manuscripts, lovingly written and illuminated in the *scriptoria*, were aimed at a limited audience of already converted clerics. As the Church increasingly exerted its authority on the secular life of the community, murals sprang up on the walls of the churches, bringing the story of Christianity to the masses. Following the lead of the early Christian painters of the Catacombs and still in the rigid grip of Byzantine formalism, church murals were carried out *a fresco*. Strict

The Entrance of Jesus into Jerusalem, Giotto di Bondone *c.*1266-1337. Giotto, who brought much of the quality of Gothic sculpture to his work, was to change the whole course of European painting (Scrovegni Chapel, Padua)

rules governed the contents of these paintings. Artists were restricted to preordained, symbolic colours and gestures.

In the 13th century a group of painters in Italy gradually broke away from the rigidity of this highly conventionalized art. These painters, turning to the art of the late Classical era, arrived at a personal style that would appeal to and overawe the viewers. The most influential of these innovators was Cenni di Peppo, known as Cimabue. He introduced a degree of realism and solidity of form that anticipated Giotto, who was to have a major effect on Western art.

The technique of fresco, used, albeit unconsciously, by Cro-Magnon hunter artists, is the oldest form of painting in a water-bound medium. Later, the Egyptians, Greeks and Romans consciously used the technique, which in its purest form has great lasting qualities; under favourable conditions, the colours retain their luminosity and intensity indefinitely. Cennino Cennini, in his *Libro dell' Arte*, a treatise on technique written at the turn of the 15th century, explains that in true fresco, 'the sweetest and subtlest technique that exists', the artist must apply his pigment directly on to damp, fresh (*fresco*)

Rucellai Madonna. Cimabue, 1240-1302
(Uffizi Gallery, Florence)

plaster. The colour, penetrating the wet plaster and becoming part of it, dries to a rock-hard amalgam. This is brought about by the chemical action of the calcium hydroxide in the wet plaster combining with the carbon dioxide in the atmosphere to form calcium carbonate. The technique was used during the golden age of Italian wall painting from Cimabue to Michelangelo. It called for great skill, confidence and decisiveness. The painter could only tell from experience how the final colour of his work would turn out; as the contemporary art historian, Vasari, wrote: 'When the wall is wet, the colours on it do not look the same as they do when it is dry.' Once the pigment was applied it was instantly sucked into the plaster.

Later, a faster method of fresco was devised. By painting on dry (*secco*) plaster, the painter had full control of his colour and could rectify any mistakes. The overall time taken was considerably shorter. This method required a binding medium; usually, glue, egg (for tempera), or oil was mixed with the pigment to ensure that it adhered to the surface of the wall. Although quicker, painting *a secco* lost much of the quality of true fresco, causing Michelangelo to remark indignantly, 'Oil painting is for women, and slow and slovenly people.' Presented with already dry plaster on the altar wall of the Sistine Chapel, on which he was to paint his *Last Judgement*, he demanded it be removed so he could work *a fresco*.

The technical preparation for true fresco as described by Cennini was carried out by the artist himself. A layer of coarse plaster, the *arriccio*, was trowelled directly on to the wall, its surface left uneven to act as a key for the upper layer of fine plaster, the *intonaco* – 'so well slaked that it has the appearance of an ointment'. It was spread 'thin, but not too thin and perfectly flat'. A fine cord soaked in red paint was stretched taut down the middle of the wall, then plucked, to make a central guide line. Should the space be large, this was repeated to give a number of vertical and horizontal divisions. The artist went to great trouble to work out his theme on the *arriccio*. First drawing in the outline of the composition in charcoal, he went over this in pale ochre, using a fine, pointed brush – the surplus charcoal being flicked away with a bunch of feathers. The drawing was finally retraced with 'sinopia' red, from which it derives its name.

Working from the top – the very large frescoes needed scaffolding, which had to be lowered as the artist worked down the wall – the

Overleaf: *The Annunciation.* Fra Angelico (St Mark's, Florence)

Christ appearing to the Apostles. Duccio di Buoninsegna, d.1319 (Opera del Duomo, Siena)

ANTE FIGVRAM PRETEREVNDO CAVE NE SILEATVR AVE

Above: *Marchese Ludovico Gonzaga meeting his son.* Andrea Mantegna, 1423-1457 (Ducal Palace, Mantua)

artist spread on a section of *intonaco*, enough to last him a day, painting from first light to evening. This *giornata* ('day's work') was large or small according to the complexity of the work to be carried out on a particular day. Later, full-sized cartoons, squared up with a *rete* (net), were used, the design being pricked through into the wet *intonaco* with a needle. With masterly sureness of touch, the artist began his painting, section by section, the *intonaco* applied to overlap slightly the previous day's work.

The Florentine painter Cimabue (1240–*c*1302) and his contemporary Pietro Cavallini (*fl*1270–1330) brought vitality, a sense of naturalism through modelling and a simple application of the principles of perspective to the art of fresco. Even more important, they imbued their work with atmosphere and feeling. Duccio di Buoninsegna (*d*1319) and his pupil Simone Martini (*c*1282–1344), working in tempera, increased the narrative content and introduced figures that were believable. But it was Giotto di Bondone (*c*1266–1337) who was to change the whole course of European painting.

Giotto brought much of the quality of Gothic sculpture to his paintings. Through the use of modelling and deep shadow, his figures became solid and statuesque, existing in an illusion of space and depth; they were real people, doing real things. A greater innovation was his ability to convey emotion through expression and movement. In his painting, *The Mourning of Christ*, probably completed in 1306, the Virgin crouches grief-stricken over the still body of Christ; St John,

Below: *The Flagellation of Christ.* Piero della Francesca *c.*1420-1492 (Ducal Palace, Urbino)

flinging out his arms in an instinctive gesture, creates a sensation of utter despair. Although conventionalized angels float about in a formal sky, the main figures are all too believably real. Giotto, breaking away from the Oriental concept that each figure should be shown in its entirety, superimposes one upon another, masterly conveying a sense of space between St John and the crouching, back-view figures in the foreground who, although their faces are hidden, nevertheless convey a sense of tragic grief.

Following Giotto, the painters of the Renaissance added new dimensions to fresco painting as the New Learning began to influence the visual arts. Masaccio (1401–28), Mantegna (1423–57), Piero della Francesca (c1420–92), Paolo Uccello (1397–1475), Andrea del Castagno (1423–57) and Pisanello (1395–1455) all added their personal contributions to fresco painting; freed from stultifying convention, they were able to express themselves as individuals.

The art of painting *a fresco*, as opposed to *a secco* reached its height in the work of Michelangelo Buonarroti (1475–1564). Through his studies of Giotto, Masaccio, and Classical sculptures, and through his research into human anatomy, Michelangelo represented the human body in all its beauty and mobility. Persuaded by Pope Sixtus IV, much against his will, to decorate the vault of the Sistine Chapel, Michelangelo reluctantly shut himself away and, allowing no one near him, began the frescoes which ever since have amazed the whole world. This has remained one of the great masterpieces of all time in its grandeur of vision, its wealth of new invention and its execution of detail. It was painted while he lay on his back, looking upwards. (He got so used to this cramped position that he held letters, received during this period, above his head and bent backwards to read them.)

Despite Michelangelo's fierce championing of true fresco, artists of the period, inundated with commissions, turned to working *a secco* for speed and in doing so lost much of the quality of the fresco painting which made the Italian Renaissance an era of unsurpassed artistic achievement.

Overleaf: *The Creation.* A panel from the ceiling of the Sistine Chapel. Michelangelo Buonarroti, 1475-1564

Below: *Christ with the Apostles.* Masaccio 1410-1428 (Sta Maria del Carmine, Florence)

'Painters in Little'

Miniature painting is believed by most authorities to have stemmed from the art of illumination – a direct development of the small drawings and paintings that were used to decorate bibles, books of hours and missals. The word miniature is derived from the Latin *minium*, the word for red lead, the pigment used to paint initial letters on medieval illuminated manuscripts. Although popularly regarded as a small, jewel-like object to be worn, a miniature is in fact defined as a painted portrait that can be easily held in the hand. Consequently they range in size up to 10 or 11 in., or 25–30 cm. The *Three Brothers Browne*, painted in 1598, measures 9⅞ in. × 11¾ in. (25.1 × 29.9 cm) and a number of others are even larger. Those to be worn, the ornamental miniatures, are usually circular or oval in shape, while

Hans Holbein, 1497/8-1543, introduced the art of miniature painting into England. His portrait of Mrs Pemberton *(bottom)* has all the qualities of a major painting but his miniature of Anne of Cleves was flattering and infuriated Henry VIII (Victoria and Albert Museum, London)

cabinet miniatures, those to be framed and displayed, are sometimes rectangular. Until the mid-17th century these portraits were known as limnings or 'painting in little'.

In the 16th century miniatures were usually painted on vellum, the skin scraped down as thinly as possible and mounted on a paste board. In his *The Gentleman's Exercise*, written at the beginning of the 17th century, Henry Peacham (1576–1649) writes, 'Take of the fairest and smoothest pastboard you can get, which with a sleeke stone rubbe as smooth, and as even as you can, that done, take the fine skin of an Abortive, which you may buy in Paternoster Row, and other places, (it being the finest parchment that is) and with a starch thinne laid on, and the skin well stretched . . . prepare your ground and tablet, then according to the generall complexion of the face you are to draw, lay on a weake colour, that done, trace out the eyes, nose, mouth and eare, with lake or red Lead, and if the complexion is swarthy, adde either of Sea coale, lampe black to deepen and shadow it. . .' He goes on, '. . . then little by little, worke it with a curious hand with the lively colour, till you have brought it to perfection.'

'Lively' the colours certainly were. Often painted against bright blue backgrounds, the portraits glow with life, the ornate Tudor costume standing out rich and distinct. The early miniature painters had a wide palette of mineral and vegetable pigments which they ground down themselves to an extremely fine powder. The powder was then 'washed': as one artist wrote, '. . . this is effected by putting the ground color into a bason of water, and letting it stand a few minutes, pouring the top gently off into a second vessel, and letting that stand double or triple the time of the former; then into a third; and so on . . . each time will afford a finer sediment'. The dry powders were stored in small ivory containers. When required, they were mixed with powdered gum and sugar candy or honey and dissolved in hot water. These brilliant, opaque colours, applied as gouache, have retained their luminosity to this day.

Hans Holbein (1497–1543) introduced the art of miniature painting into England in 1526. It rapidly became the vogue at the glittering court of Henry VIII and remained popular throughout the reign of his daughter, Elizabeth I. Many other European countries were already producing beautiful miniature portraits, but the medium had a particular appeal to English court artists. The atmosphere of extravagance, of finery and artifice, of intrigue and dalliance at the English court provided a perfect setting for the growth of 'portraits in little'. Courtiers had their likenesses copied to be worn by their lovers. Henry VIII insisted on true likenesses being painted on diplomatic documents, and numerous miniatures of Elizabeth I were sent by her to her admirers and suitors.

Holbein, on the recommendation of Erasmus, was taken up by Sir Thomas More when he arrived in England and for a number of years he lived at the Chelsea home of Henry VIII's chancellor. His portraits of Sir Thomas and his family remain among the best of his work. Persuaded by the King to reside at court, Holbein painted several royal portraits as well as numerous courtiers. In 1539, he was sent abroad to paint a likeness of Anne of Cleves, whom Thomas Cromwell had proposed as Henry's next wife. Holbein's circular miniature of her (all his miniatures were round; the oval shape appeared towards the end of the century) is only 1¾ in. (4.5 cm) in diameter but is probably his most successful limning. Painted against an intense blue background, the head-and-shoulders portrait displays a remarkable treatment of material and decoration, the painting of the lace and muslin unbelievably fine. With little trace of light and shade, the face depicted is that of an attractive young woman with a healthy

Above: Self portrait, painted at the age of thirty. Nicholas Hilliard, 1547-1619 (Victoria and Albert Museum, London)

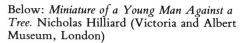

Below: *Miniature of a Young Man Against a Tree*. Nicholas Hilliard (Victoria and Albert Museum, London)

clear skin. There can be no doubt that the portrait was flattering, for on seeing his future wife, Henry VIII was severely disappointed.

Miniature painting reached its peak during the reign of Elizabeth I, when Nicholas Hilliard (1547–1619) and his pupil Isaac Oliver produced a stream of dazzling portraits. Hilliard, son of an Exeter goldsmith, was apprenticed to another jeweller and goldsmith, becoming a freeman of the Goldsmiths' Company in 1569. At the early age of thirteen he was already painting miniatures. There exists a self-portrait dated 1560 and precociously inscribed in gilt, OPERA QVEDAM IPIVS NICHOLAIS HELIARD IN AETATIS SUAE, though it does not compare in quality with the self-portrait of 1577.

At some time before 1572 Hilliard was appointed 'Limner & Goldsmith' to the Queen, but life was not always easy under royal patronage. Drawn to use shadows to suggest relief, he was sternly lectured by Elizabeth: the Italians, she said, who 'had the name to be cunningest and to drawe best shadowed not'. She insisted on sitting for him in the 'open ally of a goodly garden where no tree was neere nor any shadow at all. . .' Ever compliant, Hilliard wrote afterwards, 'This Her Majesties curiouse demand, hath greatly bettered my judgement.' He went on to make portraits of many of the great figures of the Elizabethan age: Drake, Raleigh, Leicester, Mary Queen of Scots, Lady Arabella Stewart and countless others. He is perhaps

Below: *Two Little Girls aged 4 and 5.* Isaac Oliver, d.1617 (Victoria and Albert Museum, London)

Below right: *Portrait of a Young Man,* Isaac Oliver (Copyright reserved. Reproduced by gracious permission of Her Majesty Queen Elizabeth II)

remembered best for two particular masterpieces, *An Unknown Youth* (5½ × 2¾ in. or 14 × 7 cm), which is believed by some to be the youthful Robert Devereux, earl of Essex, and George Clifford, earl of Cumberland (10⅛ × 7 in. or 25.8 × 17.8 cm) painted around 1590.

Hilliard was no mere copyist, as he explains in his *Arte of Limning*, written about 1600. He advises the 'curious drawer' to watch and capture 'these lovely graces, witty smilings, and these stolen glances which suddenly like lightning, pass and another countenance taketh place.' To note carefully '. . . how the eye changeth and narroweth . . . the nostrils play and are more open, the veins in the temple appear more and colour by degrees increaseth . . . how the eyebrows make the straight arches.'

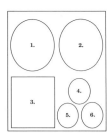

1. *Richard Whitmore*. Bernard Lens, 1682-1740
2. *Katherine Whitmore*. Bernard Lens
3. *Queen Charlotte*. Samuel Finney, 1718/19-1798
4. *Peg Woffington*. A. B. Lens, 1713-1779
5. *Unknown Boy*. Thomas Redmond, 1745-1785
6. *Unknown Woman*. P. P. Lens, 1714-1750
(Victoria and Albert Museum, London)

Hilliard's pupil Isaac Oliver (1556–1617) was brought to England by his father, a Huguenot goldsmith, to escape religious persecution in Rouen. Oliver learned the art of limning from Hilliard and continued in the same tradition, but by 1595 he was rivalling the master and some of his miniatures of about that date compare favourably with those of Hilliard. On the death of Elizabeth, the subtleties of painting which she insisted upon from Hilliard died with her. James I and his court favoured the more realistic approach of Oliver, who achieved his accurate likenesses with the use of shadows.

James II as Duke of York. Samuel Cooper, 1609-1672 (Victoria and Albert Museum, London)

During the 17th century, the greater attention paid to perspective and anatomical facial structure led to more lifelike portraits. Samuel Cooper (1609–72), more than any other artist, was responsible for this improvement in draughtsmanship. His three-quarter portrait of *James, Duke of York*, afterwards King James II ($3\frac{1}{4} \times 2\frac{5}{8}$ in. or 8.3×6.7 cm) clearly shows the move away from Elizabethan miniature painting. The colour is more restrained, the background subdued, with a suggestion of cloud effect; gone are the elaborately gilded inscriptions of Nicholas Hilliard and the Elizabethans. Cooper also devised a method of laying a ground of white paint on his vellum before beginning his painting.

Miniature painting reached a wider clientele during the 18th century, when innumerable artists worked in the medium yet were stretched to meet the demand. By then other materials were replacing vellum: ivory, enamel and even porcelain. Among the many successful miniature painters of the period, Richard Cosway (c1742–1821) was probably the most gifted, and his work contributed to the popular expansion of miniature painting in the late 18th century. With the advent of photography, the popularity of the miniature portrait waned, although even today there are a few artists specializing in this art.

13

Dürer:
Father of European Watercolour

'For in truth, art is implicit in nature, and whoever can extract it has it.' These words of Albrecht Dürer (1471–1528) sum up the painter's attitude towards his work; his insatiable thirst for knowledge, his acute powers of observation and his painstaking efforts to record what he had seen.

Born at Nuremberg in 1471, the son of a master goldsmith from Hungary, Dürer grew up in that singular period in European history when the widening of cultural horizons laid the foundation for modern Europe. Gothic concepts in the north were already giving way to the Renaissance sweeping up from the south. The spread of humanism and the 'New Learning' was facilitated by the invention of printing; books setting out the ideas of Italian poets, philosophers and painters flowed across the Alps into northern Europe. In Germany, the discontented rumblings within the Church, escalating towards the

The Great Piece of Turf. Albrecht Dürer, 1471-1528. To Dürer each individual leaf, each blade of grass or half-opened flower held its own religious essence. Watercolour and gouache (Albertina, Vienna)

Reformation, greatly increased social and political tensions.

Dürer was drawn to humanism and the concept that a contemplation of beauty gave man a glimpse of the spiritual world beyond earthly experience: To Dürer, each individual leaf, each blade of grass or half-opened flower, as depicted for instance in his watercolour study of *The Great Piece of Turf*, painted in 1502, held its own religious essence. 'What is painting?' he once wrote. 'To paint is to portray upon a flat surface any visible thing whatsoever.' And to Dürer, 'Sight is the noblest sense of man.'

On leaving school Dürer became an apprentice in his father's workshop, but the craft of the goldsmith was not for him; he had to paint. With no little difficulty, he persuaded his father to release him from his articles – an almost unheard-of occurrence in those days – and apprentice him to the Nuremberg painter, Michael Wolgemut, for three years. His fellow apprentices may have thought him too precocious, for he wryly noted, 'During that time God granted me diligence so that I learned well, though I had to endure much from the shop boys.' In between studio chores – grinding pigments, preparing grounds and cleaning brushes – he drew, engraved on wood and learned the art of handling a brush. At this he became so skilful that, in later years, the great Venetian master Giovanni Bellini begged him for one of the special brushes he used for painting several hairs at one stroke. Dürer offered the pick of his brushes, which were exactly the same as Bellini himself used. The old Italian master, unconvinced, insisted that Dürer should there and then demonstrate his incredible brush control; which he did, drawing some long wavy tresses of a woman's hair, to the astonishment of the older man.

His earliest watercolours date from his apprenticeship in Wolgemut's workshop: *Three Linden Trees* and *The Cemetery of St John's*. Although clumsy in comparison to his later work, for he had not then gained mastery over perspective, they nevertheless indicate his ripening artistic talent. There is a sensitive use of colour, a thoroughness of detail and more than a hint of the ability to create a mood that was to become such a powerful feature of his later watercolour studies. Even at that early age, his concern with textures was apparent in his treatment of stone, brick, timber and foliage.

After returning from his *Wanderjahre*, the period of travel undertaken by young German artists and craftsmen at the completion of their apprenticeship, he married Agnes Frey in 1494. However, his travels had fired the imagination of the twenty-three-year-old Dürer; more and more he had become aware that the full realization of his own art lay in Italy. In the autumn of 1494, less than two months after his marriage, he set out for Venice, leaving his young wife behind in Nuremberg.

Very little eluded the painter's eye during the leisurely month he

Overleaf: *Wehlsch Pirg* (an Alpine scene) captures the feeling of a bright spring morning; its bold sure washes show a startling modernity (Ashmolean Museum, Oxford)

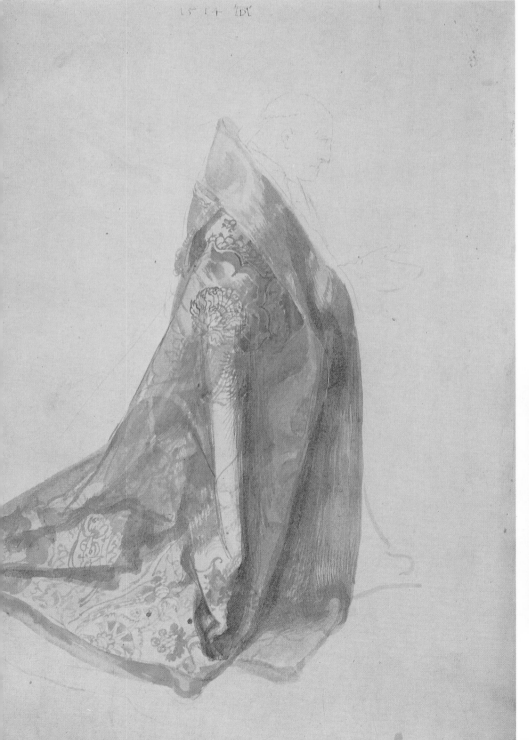

Left: Dürer made this study for the mantle of the Pope to be used in his *The Feast of the Rose-Garlands* (Albertina, Vienna)

Below: *The Feast of the Rose-Garlands*. (National Gallery, Prague)

73

Above: Dürer's drawing of a lion is a more romantic treatment of the beast than his closely observed hare, painted in infinite detail (Kunsthalle, Hamburg)

Above right: *Arco.* More detailed than his Alpine landscape, this clearly shows the influence of Giovanni Bellini (Louvre, Paris)

spent wandering through the Alps on the way to Venice. And overwhelmed by the rugged mountain scenery, forever stopping to make studies in pen and watercolour of whatever attracted his eye, he saw the Alps 'acting as a mighty ferment'. The profound effect they had upon him is captured in the surely executed watercolour landscapes he made in the misty, September light of the mountains. Many of these studies were later used as backgrounds in his paintings and engravings.

The time he spent in Venice broadened the young German's outlook on painting and composition. He learned among other things that in art a landscape is a unity greater than its parts; that lesson was to stand him in good stead for the rest of his working life. Assiduously he filled sketchbook after sketchbook with notes of the varied, teeming life of the city. Two watercolour studies of this time show his astonishing powers of observation and meticulous attention to detail. Both are of shellfish, a crab and a lobster, strange marine creatures rarely seen in his native Nuremberg. The rendering of the *Sea Crab*, correct in every detail, is made with a loving precision that far transcends mere copying. Each joint, each claw, each subtle change of colour and contour is expressed with a clarity that was to have a marked influence on the work of later naturalist painters.

His return to Nuremberg in the spring of 1475 was as leisurely as his journey out. The watercolours he made clearly reflect his new understanding of landscape. The treatment of *Wehlsch Pirg* (an Alpine scene, perhaps of the Valle di Cembra) is reminiscent of the backgrounds of Giovanni Bellini, and is an exception rather than the rule. Instead of using local colour, a characteristic of his previous work, Dürer, restricting himself to greens, blues and a pale translucent brown to suggest the earth, miraculously captures the feeling of a bright spring morning. Applied with bold, sure washes it shows a startling modernity; only the hill itself is carefully rendered in detail and heightened with body colour.

Back in Nuremberg, Dürer applied his new understanding of landscape to paintings of his native countryside. Although more detailed in treatment than *Wehlsch Pirg*, the *Weirehaus* (a small country house surrounded by water which he subsequently used as a background for his engraving, *Virgin and Child with a Monkey*), like his Alpine landscape, captures a particular time and light. It is evening, the air is still; the house is clearly reflected in the unruffled water of the lake; the absence of people and the empty boat in the foreground convey a sense of loneliness. As there is no evidence of any preliminary drawing, it would seem that Dürer, having first laid on the basis of the composition with a series of direct, transparent washes, then worked up the detail in body colour applied with the dexterity so admired by Giovanni Bellini.

Some of Dürer's watercolours strongly emphasize his preoccupation with engraving. In these, the drawing totally dominates the study, the colour being reduced to a series of tints. In the *Nuremberg Woman Dressed for Church*, the colour added has the quality of a woodcut. The *Virgin with a Multitude of Animals* (1503), a pen and black ink drawing tinted with colour washes, has a homeliness missing in the Classical Italian nativities. Here the Virgin is surrounded by the birds and animals that so delighted Dürer, each drawn with loving accuracy.

Dürer's love of nature is best conveyed by his studies of animals and plants. Probably his best known watercolour study is the *Young Hare*, painted in 1502. First laying broad washes of colour to achieve the outline of the animal, he used a fine brush to pick out the hair with body colour, finally touching in the highlights with white. Although drawn with incredible accuracy in microscopic detail, the animal lives: the viewer feels that at any moment it will twitch its whiskers or flick its ears. No less appealing, though less well known, is the *Head of a Roe Deer*. Here Dürer's control of fine brush strokes is near miraculous, and although limited to browns and greys, the animal is completely lifelike.

Although Dürer's watercolours represent only a fraction of his output, he can truly be regarded as the forerunner of the great English watercolour movement. It is a matter for speculation how much he would have achieved had he concentrated on watercolour alone.

Although painstakingly accurate, this painting of a hare has all the life and vitality of the real animal (Albertina, Vienna)

14

The Rise of Watercolour in England

Between the death of Dürer in 1528 and the beginning of its great revival in the early years of the 18th century, watercolour became virtually a forgotten art. Its revival is a unique phenomenon in the history of Western art, which at its height coincided with the Industrial Revolution and became an important manifestation of Romanticism, yet was curiously confined almost exclusively to England until the mid-19th century. As a particularly English art, watercolour had its roots in the work of the monastic illustrators of the *Lindisfarne Gospels* and the *Book of Kells*. That work had influenced the rise and eager acceptance of the miniature in the 16th century. Yet the art of 'painting in little' had to be reintroduced into the country from the continent by Holbein. A similar situation was to arise in the case of watercolour landscape painting as an art form.

The grandiose claims of 18th- and 19th-century art historians ('Painting in watercolours may justly be regarded as a new art, and its present application the invention of British artists', or 'the growth in Britain of the truly national art, known as drawing or painting in watercolours. . .') were not accurate. True, it was in England that artists saw its possibility as a medium and extended it to full maturity as an art form in its own right; but watercolour painting had no spontaneous, miraculous birth there.

Albrecht Dürer, working both in gouache and transparent watercolour to produce meticulous naturalistic studies of animals and

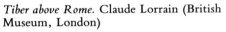

Tiber above Rome. Claude Lorrain (British Museum, London)

Papauer siluestris   Coquelicot.

A.M.3267 b — '56.   V. A. M.

plants and sweeping views of Alpine scenery that anticipated the later English topographers and Romantics, had led the way. He also anticipated the use of local colour, which was to become so important a feature of the work of Girtin, Turner, Constable, Cox and Cotman. He advised, 'Be careful that thou shade each colour with a similar colour. Thus I hold that a yellow, to retain its kind, must be shaded with yellow, darker toned than the principal colour. . . Happen what may every colour must in shading keep to its own class.'

Dürer was no isolated instance. Artists throughout Europe were employing watercolour as a medium, either in studies for oils or as an immediate record of a scene that caught their fancy, though they mainly used it only to tint pen, pencil or chalk sketches. Monochrome was in general use and, in the hands of such masters as Claude Lorrain and Rembrandt, a bistre (a brown pigment made from charred wood) landscape could not only take on a sense of light and space but miraculously suggest an intense colour contrast. When colour was used, particularly by 17th-century Dutch artists such as Ostade,

79

Above: *The Tower of London*. Wenceslaus Hollar, 1607-1677 (British Museum, London)

Below: *The River at Hampton Court*. Sir James Thornhill, 1675-1734 (Whitworth Art Gallery, University of Manchester)

Cuyp, Hans Bol and Avercamp, it was highly tentative, used to pick out particular points in a drawing. Rarely was it superimposed to convey a sense of depth and variety; the drawing would stand complete without it. Colour was used as a note: a limited palette of yellow, green and brown added interest to the foreground; a touch of blue enhanced the sky. Never was it used for its own sake or to express a mood.

The Dutch artists worked in both transparent tints and gouache. The latter medium, always more popular on the continent, nevertheless played its part in the English watercolour movement.

Landscape art, still alien in England at the beginning of the 17th century, was eventually to become the main theme of the watercolour. Two main traditions influenced this development: Italian Classicism and Dutch realism. The 17th-century Italian style developed by Annibale Carracci, Albani and later by the Frenchmen, Nicolas Poussin and Claude Lorrain, used landscape as a setting for mythological and historical scenes. It is generalized, conceptual landscape rather than a naturalistic treatment of detail which frames a

central vista bathed in diffused sunlight. On the other hand, the Dutch approach to landscape was naturalistic, perceptual. Other painters – Breughel, Rembrandt – and other influences had their effect, but it was these two traditions that influenced the English watercolourists.

Even towards the end of the 16th century, when watercolour in the hands of Nicholas Hilliard, Isaac Oliver and others was directed to the production of courtly miniatures, isolated artists were using it for other purposes. When Sir Richard Grenville, of the *Revenge*, sailed with seven ships in 1585 to found the first English colony in America, one of the adventurers who accompanied him was John White, who made fascinating watercolour studies of the country and its flora and fauna (see Chapter 28). Another artist working in watercolour at this time was Jacques le Moyne de Morgues, a Frenchman born in Dieppe who escaped to England at the time of the St Bartholomew Massacre (1572). Le Moyne is chiefly known for his studies of flowers and fruit in 16th-century English gardens. Executed in pure watercolour here and there picked out with touches of gouache, these drawings show an exactness of detail comparable with the botanical paintings of the 19th century: their colours appear as fresh as the day they were painted. Inigo Jones (1573–1652), the architect, was also using watercolour in his sketches for the court masques of Ben Jonson.

When Peter Paul Rubens went as ambassador to the court of Charles I in 1629, he took with him a taste for landscape painting, 'soe new in England', He had been painting in watercolour for some twenty years and soon interested the King in the medium, as this extract from a royal inventory shows.

A landskape with water cullours	£ 2. 0. 0.
A picture in water cullours of the beheading of the Queen of Scotts	£12. 0. 0
Spanish Fleet in 88 water colours	£ 3. 0. 0.
Tobias in water colours by ye King's Niece	£ 2. 6. 0.

Anthony van Dyck (1599–1641), who followed Rubens to London in 1632, produced a number of landscape drawings that show an ease and breadth of expression. His *Country Lane* and *A Tree-Bordered Country Lane*, depicting the fresh greens and faint blues of a summer's day in England, may be said to be the starting point of the English landscape tradition. Van Dyck's poetic quality was to be echoed in the work of Gainsborough, but he had less influence on the next generation of watercolourists. These, the advance guard of the watercolour movement, broke new ground with their 'topographical' work and laid the foundation for a continuing tradition.

In 1636, Thomas Howard, earl of Arundel, one of the first English patrons of art, sent for Wenceslaus Hollar (1607–77). Hollar, born in Prague, had already worked at Frankfurt, Cologne and Antwerp and was familiar with the various styles of watercolour drawing current in

Left: *A Rook*. Charles Collins, d.1744 (Victoria and Albert Museum, London)

Overleaf: *A Country Lane*. Anthony Van Dyck, 1599-1641. The fresh greens and faint blues of this picture, depicting an English summer's day, may be said to be the starting point of the English landscape tradition (British Museum, London)

81

A. Vandyck

Opposite: *Tivoli: The Great Cascade.* Jonathan Skelton (Victoria and Albert Museum, London)

Right: *Dropping Well, Knaresborough.* Francis Place, 1647-1728 (British Museum, London)

Europe. He married an English girl and made the country his permanent home (apart from eight years exile in Antwerp during the Commonwealth period). Hollar introduced a method of washing pale tints of transparent colour over a pen drawing, using a limited palette of blue, yellow, green, pale brown and rose madder. First and foremost a recorder, his close, accurate representation of architecture and landscape encouraged the foundation of the English topographical school of watercolour painting.

A far more imaginative artist, Francis Place (1647–1728), first met Hollar early in his career and wrote of him. 'He was a person I was intimately acquainted withal, but never his disciple nor anybody else's, which was my misfortune.' Place's attitude to his work, style and choice of subject was greatly influenced by Hollar, but his drawings were already showing the lyrical quality that was to become such a feature of 18th-century English watercolour. Hollar struggled to make a living: 'he did all by the hour in which he was very exact for if any body came in that kep him from his business he always laid ye hour glass on one side, till they were gone . . . he always recond on 12d an hour.' But Place was not financially dependent on his art, and 'travelled thro many parts of England Wales into Ireland, drew views of many places very well.' The topographical artists would follow in his footsteps, touring the British Isles with a camera obscura.

By the early years of the 18th century, more and more English artists were turning to watercolour, using it mainly for making studies, or as relaxation from what was considered the more arduous task of oil painting. But a few artists, among them William Taverner, Jonathan Skelton and Francis Cotes, were beginning to regard the medium as a means of producing finished pictures.

William Hogarth (1697–1764), the leading artist in Britain during the first half of the 18th century, usually worked in oils, but the few existing watercolours attributed to him are sensitive and finely drawn. He once made a sketching trip from London to the Isle of Sheppey in Essex, described at the time as a 'Five Days Peregrination of the Five Following Persons vizt. Messieurs Tothall, Scott, Hogarth, Thornhill & Forest. . .' The cost of the tour for the whole party was six guineas. Hogarth, when he could spare the time, worked in an academy conducted by Sir James Thornhill (1675–1734); he eventually ran away with his teacher's daughter and married her, much to her father's chagrin. Thornhill himself made hundreds of pen and wash and colour drawings of architectural decoration. His more rare landscapes and figure compositions are lively and show he must have studied Rembrandt closely.

Hilly Scene with Village and Horseman. Peter Tillemans, 1684-1734 (Yale Center for British Art, New Haven)

Another artist working at this time in watercolour and gouache was Peter Tillemans (1684–1734), a native of Antwerp. After a period spent copying oil paintings, he was employed by John Bridges to make five hundred drawings for his *History of Northamptonshire*, for which he was paid a guinea a day plus free board and lodging. Particularly in his *Landscape with Horsemen*, Tillemans' breadth of treatment is unusual for his day.

William Taverner (1703–72), the grandson of Jeremiah Taverner, a 'face painter', was a gifted amateur (he was procurator general of the Canterbury Court of Arches) who devoted all his spare time to landscape painting. Working in watercolour and gouache as well as oils, he followed closely the style of Claude and Poussin, but his watercolour landscapes – he was the first British artist to paint free landscapes systematically in the medium – are well drawn, their colour pleasing. His general method, though at times he touched in with gouache, was to tint in sepia over a pencil or chalk drawing, then add washes of colour, finally accenting the foreground in pen. He was well thought of in his day, but his obituary in the *Gentleman's Magazine*, describing him as 'one of the best landscape painters England ever produced', overstated the case.

Other landscape artists of note during this period were J. Hadley, an amateur only discovered in the 1930s who painted a number of watercolours of Hampshire and the Isle of Wight, Jonathan Skelton (c1735–1759) and Francis Cotes (1726–70). Skelton was one of the earliest artists to work in the manner of 'stained drawings', washing transparent local colour over an Indian ink monochrome underpainting; one or two of his drawings even show the direct use of local colour.

Two other artists of interest of this era are Charles Collins (d1744) and George Edwards (1694–1773). Francis Place had discovered that watercolour is the ideal medium for painting birds, and Collins and Edwards devoted their lives to ornithological studies. Collins in particular, working directly in local colour without any sign of pen work, produced some rich watercolour impressions, his colour clear and accurate.

15
The 18th-Century Romantics

The 17th-century painters from France, Germany and the Netherlands who settled in Rome had been irresistibly drawn to the grandeur of Italian scenery and the remains of Classical civilization. Nicolas Poussin's Classical landscapes, though of great beauty and high artistic merit, were orderly and perfectly composed; nature had to conform with Poussin's ideal. Claude Lorrain also composed landscapes in the Classical tradition, but made them more poetic and decorative, and consequently more appealing to aristocratic patron and foreign visitor.

Succeeding generations of artists in Italy continued in the vein of picturesque landscape established by Claude. But, working often from engravings of earlier artists, they added very little of their own natural experience, painting very much to a formula. Mountain and river became almost obligatory ingredients as did waterfall, ruined temple, tower and fallen column. This formula was to the taste of the stream of foreign collectors who flocked to Italy. From early in the 18th century, the 'Grand Tour' of the continent had become popular with the English gentry, who were becoming the major art patrons of Europe; they showed, however, a marked preference for foreign painters. By the close of the century the increasingly prosperous middle class was also taking up foreign travel – and buying pictures. In 1785, it was estimated that 40,000 English people, counting masters and servants, were travelling or living abroad. This bred a taste for the topographical watercolour, a taste which by this time was not entirely

Killarney and Lake. William Pars, 1742-1782 (Victoria and Albert Museum, London)

restricted to the continent. The 'romantic' scenery of Scotland, Wales and the Lake District was being discovered. As Wilberforce wrote in 1788, 'the banks of the Thames are scarcely more public than those of Windermere.' The word picturesque found its way into the English language to describe these paintings of wild or charming scenery.

Thus, English watercolour began to separate into two streams. One set out to make a faithful recording of a particular place or building; the other to capture the artist's personal interpretation of an aspect of nature. John Ruskin referred to the former as 'simple' or historical topography; the latter as Turnerian or poetical. We see in the latter the beginnings of the Romantic movement.

When Richard Wilson (1714–82) returned to England from Italy in 1755, he had every expectation of success. Though, like Gainsborough, essentially a painter in oils, his approach to landscape painting had a profound effect on the watercolour landscape artists who came after him. Wilson, the son of the rector of Penegoes in Montgomeryshire, was sent to London at fifteen to 'indulge his prevailing love of the arts of design', subsidized by a relative of his mother, Sir George Wynne. He spent six years in the studio of a portrait painter before setting up on his own in an expensive house near Covent Garden which at first he could ill afford. With success came a craving to go to Italy, which he did in 1750, settling first in Venice, where he spent a year, before going on to Rome. It was during his stay in Venice that Francesco Zuccarelli (1704–88) persuaded him that his true metier lay in landscape painting.

An original artist in every sense, Wilson broke away from the picturesque landscape of Claude and his successors and came, as Sir Joshua Reynolds said, 'near common nature'. Abandoning the Classical, his painting recorded a Romantic reaction to nature. It was this that so influenced Turner, Girtin, Crome and to some extent John Sell Cotman, whose watercolours manifest Wilson's influence.

Wilson painted no watercolours as independent works of art, but he did add transparent and body colour to many of his studies and sketches in pencil and chalk. Difficult, unamiable, outspoken and

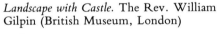

Landscape with Castle. The Rev. William Gilpin (British Museum, London)

jealously critical of his contemporaries – he spoke scathingly of Gainsborough's 'fried parsley' landscapes – he was also subject to violent fits of temper.

When serving on the hanging committee of the Royal Academy, he was known to reduce brightly coloured paintings to his own restrained colour range by painting a mixture of Indian ink and Spanish liquorice over them.

Among the few watercolours left by Wilson, and they are really tinted monochromes, is *Moonrise on a River*, a haunting, moonlit scene of a castle jutting into a lake, coloured in delicate tones of blue-grey and cream. His *Landscape*, probably a study for *The Destruction of Niobe's Children*, was for some time believed to be in thin oil on paper, but it is now accepted as a body colour sketch, for which the artist worked dry colour with size. In monochrome studies like *Torre Delle Grotte, Near Naples* and *Hermits by a Pool*, Wilson achieves a remarkable sense of colour and space with black chalk, white and a range of grey washes.

He died, embittered and poor, in 1782. His brilliance was not even given an obituary in any newspaper.

Thomas Gainsborough (1727–88) differed from Wilson and the topographical artists in a number of ways. The past held nothing for him and he had no desire to go to Italy; no urge to saturate himself in its grandeur and wander about its Classical ruins. In both style and temperament he was closer to the French painters Watteau and Fragonard. To him landscape was a relaxation from the tedium of hack work – portrait painting for the gentry. His letters make it clear that his portraits had no interest for him other than the fees he received for them. Gainsborough drew and painted with natural sensibility rather than from careful study and an intellectual searching out of form.

Thomas Gainsborough was the third of nine children of an unsuccessful cloth merchant of Sudbury. His parents, impressed by the boy's talents, sent him to London, where he became a pupil of Hubert Gravelot, the French illustrator and engraver. Three years later, in much the same way as Wilson, Gainsborough set himself up in Hatton Garden as a portrait and landscape painter. There he met an artist and man about town, Frank Hayman, who introduced him to the seedier delights of London. This must have contributed to his lack of success, for he later wrote, advising a young actor friend: 'Don't run about London streets, fancying you are catching strokes of nature, at the hazard of your constitution. It was my first school, and deeply read in petticoats I am, therefore you may allow me to caution you.'

At the age of nineteen, he married the natural daughter of the Duke of Beaufort, and her private income of two hundred pounds a year was for many years a vital source of income to the young couple. After a number of years spent in Ipswich, Gainsborough, on the advice of his friend and patron, Philip Thicknesse, sold up and moved to Bath, where commissions began to pour in – for portraits. His landscapes, greatly admired by fellow artists, rarely sold, and according to one of his friends, Gainsborough 'was so disgusted at the blind preference paid to his powers of portraiture, that for many years of his residence in Bath, he regularly shut up all his landscapes in the back apartments of his house, to which no common visitors were admitted.' In 1774, he left the West Country for London, where he stayed until his death. On his deathbed he admitted regretting the dissolute life he had led, but characteristically added, 'They must take me altogether, liberal, thoughtless and dissipated.'

Bearing in mind the work of the 19th-century naturalists' landscapes, it is difficult for modern viewers to appreciate Gainsborough as an innovator; to us his landscapes lack reality. Like the Rev. William Gilpin, he drew his inspiration 'from the general face of the country; not from any particular scene'. His native Sudbury became broadly 'Suffolk'. Oak, ash, beech and chestnut lost their individual identity and became 'trees'. Apart from his constant sketching, he seldom worked out of doors. And yet there is an interesting similarity between remarks made by Constable and this of Gainsborough, recorded by his friend Thicknesse, 'that during his boy-hood, though he had no idea of becoming a Painter then, yet there was not a picturesque clump of trees, nor even a tree of beauty, no, nor hedge row, stone or post, at the corner of the lanes, for some miles round about the place of his nativity, that he had not so perfectly in his mind's eye, that had he known he could use a pencil, he could have perfectly delineated.'

There is a grain of truth in Wilson's scathing remark about 'fried parsley'. Of an evening, Gainsborough would compose 'thoughts for the landscape scenery' on a 'little old-fashioned folding oak table . . .

The Lake of Albano and Castel Gandolfo. John Robert Cozens, 1752-1799 (Yale Center for British Art, New Haven)

held sacred for the purpose'. These consisted of pieces of cork, coal or broken stones for the foreground; sand, bits of mirror and clay for the middle ground; bushes of moss and lichen, and distant woods of broccoli. These, as Reynolds wrote, 'he magnified and improved into rocks, trees and water.' His watercolours too are slightly theatrical. But they have a spontaneous charm and clarity of colour that influenced many of his contemporaries.

Gainsborough may have been hasty and impatient, but he was one of the greatest draughtsmen of his age and went to infinite lengths to acquire materials that best suited his technique. Once he had set his mind on a particular pigment or paper, he would not rest until he had his hands on it. He wrote to William Jackson, composer and amateur painter, 'to say the truth of your Indigo, tis delightful, so look sharp for some more (& I'll send you a drawing).' He badgered Dodsley, the publisher of Anstey's *New Bath Guide*, to let him have several quires of the paper on which it had been printed, as it exactly suited his purpose.

In his watercolours, Gainsborough sometimes added transparent washes to a pencil outline; at other times, particularly in later studies, he painted over chalk, charcoal or Indian ink, on occasion strengthening the composition with traces of gouache. In *Lovers in a Country Lane*, a charming theatrical study, he restricted himself to light gouache, picked out with pen and ink. During the 1770s, when he, and other artists, was trying to raise the status of watercolours as exhibition works, he experimented with varnished drawings.

Gainsborough has left a detailed account of this technique in a letter he wrote to Jackson. Tightening the paper on a frame until 'it may be like a drum', he painted in 'Indian Ink shaddows', lightening the tones with 'Bristol made white lead which you buy in lumps at any house painters. . .' Dipping the painting in skimmed milk, he advised (when dry) 'tinging' it with 'sap green & Bistre, your yellows with Gall stone &c &c – when this is done, float it all over with Gum water, 3 ounces of Gum Arabic to a pint of water with a Camels pencil let that dry & varnish it 3 times with Spirit Varnish.'

A number of lesser-known artists were increasingly turning to watercolour to express themselves. William Pars (1742–82) was, along with Towne and a few others, one of the first watercolour artists to apply local colour without monochrome underpainting. He turned to Italy, Greece, Asia Minor and the Alps for his subject matter, but in his Irish watercolours, of which *Killarney and Lake* is probably the best example, he captures all the ethereal beauty of that misty isle.

John Hopner (1758–1810), George Barret (1732–84), Richard Cooper (1740–1814), George Robertson (1748–88), Philip James de Loutherbourg (1740–1812) – a thorough Romantic who painted many watercolour studies for his battle pieces in oils – and Thomas (1769–1847) and Benjamin (1776–1838) Barker, all contributed in their way to the growing popularity of watercolour as a serious medium. So did

A Country Lane. Thomas Gainsborough, 1727-1788 (British Museum, London)

the Rev. William Gilpin, but more as a writer than a painter.

Gilpin summed up the whole picturesque phase in these words: 'Within the last thirty years a taste for the picturesque has sprung up – and a course of summer travelling is now looked upon to be as essential as ever a course of spring physic was in old times. While one of the flocks of fashion migrates to the sea coast, another flies off to the mountains of Wales, to the lakes in the northern provinces, or to Scotland; some to mineralise, some to botanise, some to take views of the country – all to study the picturesque, a new science for which a new language has been formed, and for which the English have discovered a new sense in themselves, which assuredly was not possessed by their fathers. This is one of the customs to which it suits a stranger to conform. My business is to see the country – and, to confess the truth, I have myself caught something of this passion for the picturesque, from conversation, from books, and still more from the beautiful landscapes in watercolour, in which the English excel all other nations.'

There were also some less orthodox artists working in watercolours. One of the most interesting is Alexander Cozens (1717–86) who according to legend (since proved false) was the bastard son of Peter the Great by a local woman, conceived when the tsar was working in Deptford dockyard. (He was certainly born in Russia and one of his sons became a general in the Russian Army.) Cozens gained the nickname 'Blotmaster' from his random watercolour technique of making blots on paper, over which he worked up Romantic scenes. A pupil of his, Henry Angelo, described the technique: 'Cozens dashed out upon several pieces of paper a series of accidental smudges and blots in black, brown and grey, which being floated on, he impressed again upon other paper, and by exercise of his fertile imagination, and a certain degree of ingenious coaxing, converted into romantic rocks, woods, towers, steeples, cottages, rivers, fields and waterfalls. Blue and grey blots formed the mountains, clouds and skies.'

However, Alexander Cozens is best known as the father of John Robert Cozens (1752–c99), a major figure in the development of the English school of watercolour. He had more influence than any other painter on both Turner and Girtin, who as youngsters made copies of his drawings in the candle-lit apartments of Dr Monro. Constable, in a letter of 1835, wrote, 'I want to know when the younger Cozens was born; his name was John, and he was the greatest genius that ever touched landscape.'

To the younger Cozens, the view he was painting was of secondary interest; its topographical or historical value minimal. He looked at landscape with a poet's eye and his watercolours, seemingly effortless, express an awareness of the beauty of nature, rather than a representation of a given scene.

In his later work, Cozens abandoned the traditional technique of washing transparent layers of pale colour over grey or sepia monochrome tones. Starting with a white ground, he put dark colour over light. Using only a faint pencil outline, with masterly finesse he floated in low-toned colour: an infinite variety of greys, some warm with red, brown and pink, others cold with blues and greens, from powder blues to light ultramarines, subtle greens and russet pinks. (His *The Lake of Albano and Castel Gandolfo* has a spontaneous appeal that belies Cozens's careful observation and selection of tints. In its simplicity of construction and treatment of form and shadow, it shows a remarkable modernity, foreshadowing the romantic watercolours of Paul Nash.) Had he not died at such an early age, John Cozens might well have rivalled his more famous followers, Turner and Girtin, in the field of watercolour.

16

Paul Sandby:
'Real Views from Nature'

'Sandby has made such a picture! such a bard! such a headlong flood! such a Snowden! such giant oaks! such desert caves! If it is not the best picture that has been painted this century in any country I'll give up all my taste to the Bench of Bishops. . .'

These words, from a letter of William Mason, biographer, amateur art critic and friend of Sir Joshua Reynolds, were written in 1760. To modern eyes Paul Sandby's work cannot be rated so highly; he is overshadowed by younger contemporaries like Turner, Constable, Cotman, David Cox, and Peter de Wint, in their mid-twenties, by Blake, holding a one-man exhibition in the year that Mason wrote, and by Samuel Palmer, still a child. Yet Gainsborough, no mean critic, described Sandby as 'the only man of genius [who has painted] real views from Nature in this country'.

Why did contemporaries rate him so highly? The answer can be found in Sandby's approach to the medium. His more discerning colleagues saw his work as the beginning of a new tradition in

Bridge of Magnificence. Thomas Sandby, 1721-1798 (Copyright reserved. Reproduced by gracious permission of Her Majesty Queen Elizabeth II)

watercolour. Hitherto primarily a means of making preliminary studies for paintings in oils or merely a recreational pastime, with Sandby watercolour was raised to the level of an independent art form – one which came to rival oil painting in popularity. Thus Sandby laid the foundation for the English watercolour movement, which in turn influenced the watercolour of the French Romantics and, later, the Impressionists' experiments.

The Sandby brothers, Thomas (1721–98) and Paul (1725–1809), were born in Nottingham. Both showed an early talent for drawing, and left for London in their teens. In 1742 Paul joined Thomas as a draughtsman in the Military Drawing Office in the Tower of London. Thomas by then had accompanied the Duke of Cumberland on a number of his campaigns in Flanders and Scotland (where he made a sketch of the battlefield of Culloden). A self-taught painter and architect, Thomas Sandby's pictures show a predilection for buildings, which are often represented almost as architectural elevations. Usually devoid of figures – unless added by his brother Paul – his wide, meticulously drawn views were made on vast sheets of paper.

When Cumberland was appointed Ranger of Windsor Great Park in 1746, he took Thomas Sandby with him as Deputy Ranger. There he spent much of his time designing and constructing the artificial lake at Virginia Water, which the Duke of Cumberland paid for out of his own pocket, to give work to the men who served under him.

After the unsuccessful rebellion of 1745 Paul Sandby was engaged in the military survey of the Highlands. During the next four or five years, to relieve the monotony of his military work he began sketching landscapes and figures. His watercolour *Draw Well at Broughton, near Edinburgh* shows that by 1751 he was already an

Above: *An Ancient Beech Tree.* Paul Sandby, 1725-1809 (Victoria and Albert Museum, London)

Overleaf: *Draw Well at Broughton, near Edinburgh.* Paul Sandby. This early watercolour of 1751 shows that the younger Sandby was already an accomplished artist and brilliant figure draughtsman (British Museum, London)

95

A View of Windsor Forest. Paul Sandby
(Victoria and Albert Museum, London)

accomplished artist and brilliant figure draughtsman. Assisted by an Edinburgh engraver named Bell, he took up etching and completed a series of Scottish views which later enjoyed something of a vogue in London. At last, wearying of surveyor's drawings, he moved south to live with his brother in Windsor Great Park.

By 1753 Paul Sandby was sufficiently well known and respected in London art circles to become involved in the controversial movement to create an art academy, a forerunner of the Incorporated Society of Artists which in 1768 became the Royal Academy of Arts with a royal charter from George III. At a meeting held at the Turk's Head Tavern in Greek Street, London, Paul Sandby was one of the committee of twenty-four elected to establish the Academy. He also published a number of scathing satirical etchings directed against Hogarth, a fierce opponent of the Academy.

Sandby's inclination toward etching is apparent in his earlier watercolours, but the criticism that these were merely pen drawings washed with colour is unfair. True, he began his paintings, after the manner of the day, by drawing his outline in a fine and even line, an etcher's line; but the infinite gradations of colour were an essential part of the painting. Though he washed in his tones first, and applied local colour last of all, he did not always limit himself to the even greys obtained by diluting Indian ink. In some of his best works the shadows are tinted with blues and pinks and blend with the restricted pallette of his local colour which, although rich and varied, is never excessively bright. Each colour was laid on and allowed to dry before the next one was glazed over it; this gave an overall uniformity to the picture, enabling the artist to control with accuracy the tonal range between foreground and background. He never used broken colour, the blurring of one colour into another. This was to come later as naturalism began to play a more significant part in the art of watercolour painting.

At first glance Sandby's watercolours appear flat and two-dimensional, but closer study shows an infinite subtlety of tone and colour. He was always experimenting with his technique, notably in his treatment of trees – Girtin had not yet demonstrated how foliage could be massed simply, to create an effect. But for all his innovations, Sandby was a conventional artist of his time. There are no strong effects of light and shade in his work, always a soft, even quality associated with an English summer's day, and essentially he was a topographical landscape artist.

However, Sandby's work falls into two main styles. His formal, Classical style, in which he carefully composes temples and ruins among stylized trees, against a background of mountains or hills, was strongly influenced by the paintings of Claude Lorrain and Poussin (as were most of his contemporaries). This style of work, much in demand among cultured patrons, was usually executed in gouache or distemper (see below). In his transparent watercolours, in many cases painted for his own enjoyment, Sandby abandons the Classical style and follows the lead of the painters of the naturalistic Dutch school, looking at his subject matter with an eye alive to and informed by nature. These simpler paintings are more deeply imaginative than his formal ones – though Sandby himself probably never thought so.

He used two distinct methods when painting in opaque body colour: gouache, in which the pigment was ground in gum and water and mixed with Chinese white, and distemper, similar to the tempera of the early Renaissance.

He was always a deeply thoughtful painter: nothing was too much trouble if it achieved the effect he wanted.

His work may not have been spontaneous, but it was certainly thorough. A friend described the extraordinary pains Paul Sandby took when executing a distemper painting. Having pinned his pasteboard to a drawing board, he flooded it with a wash of isinglass jelly mixed with a little honey. When this was nearly dry he applied an all-over wash of azure 'composed of verditer, common powder blue, and white'. He used a soft 'hog's hair tool' to paint 'pretty thick' towards the top of the picture, and diluted it with more isinglass as he approached the horizon and lighter parts of the sky. Everything below the horizontal line was painted (in azure) with a good body of colour. Next he laid in the seat of the sun with yellow ochre and white diluted with gin, melting it gradually into the azure (previously dry) by adding more gin. Then he sketched in the design. With a neutral tint, made from Prussian blue, Indian ink, white and isinglass, he 'proceeded to shadow the picture exactly as is done in forming transparent drawings, making the tint thin with gin, sometimes adding a little gum water'.

The completed underpainting, in a range of tones of the prepared neutral tint (and including a tree in leaf in the foreground), was then allowed to dry overnight. The following day he added the local colour, 'beginning in the distance, in which his greens were formed of Naples yellow, verditer and suchlike semi-transparent colours, and in proportion, as he advanced nearer the foreground, added brown ochre, sap green, and any strong colour that suited his purpose.' At this stage the painting, dead and lifeless, 'had that sort of appearance which an artist would gladly conceal from those who are unversed in painting.' The next day he brought the picture to life. In the distance, blue shadows were added, using a mixture of Prussian blue, verditer and lake, thinned down with white; 'next came the plump touches in the lights of white mixed with the local colour: these which form the heightening of the dead colouring (not laid in masses), gave astonishing light to the picture . . . then came the sharp touches of bistre.' Finally, Sandby put in his figures: 'these being sketched in with pencil, he shadowed with darker colour, quite transparent (using no Indian ink tint in those quite in front), and then add thick white in the lights and upon them the local colours . . . and worked up the whole to effect by treacle-brown and other strong colours.'

Paul Sandby, the last and possibly the best of the topographers, may not have been in the highest sense a great artist. But he above all others gave to watercolour painting what at the time it so badly needed – an independent status as an art form.

Country Girl. Paul Sandby (Copyright reserved. Reproduced by gracious permission of Her Majesty Queen Elizabeth II)

17

The Topographers

Besides Sandby, what may be called the topographical school included a number of artists whose work, long neglected, has achieved greater prominence in recent years – and higher prices at auctions.

'Scenes, situations, antiquities' – the poet Thomas Gray on a visit to the Lake District in 1769 captured the essence of the topographical school of painting in those three words. By the last quarter of the 18th century, art patrons who had travelled abroad were demanding paintings of the buildings and places they had seen on their travels, and this growing appreciation of architecture and scenery was no longer confined to Italian marbles and Alpine views. The early topographical watercolour painters hastened to depict views of the British countryside and – with the advent of sea bathing and the seaside resort – the sea. Since Elizabethan times, the English gentry had been in the habit of commissioning artists, usually itinerant painters who travelled on foot from manor to manor, to make faithful copies of their houses and estates, and the late 18th-century topographers provided a natural continuation of this tradition.

Topographic or descriptive art became all the rage and means were sought to bring such paintings before a wider public than wealthy collectors and dilettante travellers. Engravings were made from an original watercolour and then hand-coloured by girls who became expert in the craft. In 1774 Josiah Wedgwood's Staffordshire pottery produced a complete table service for Catherine the Great of Russia which was decorated with English landscapes. Fired in enamel of 'delicate black, which permits a shading and finish' on fine creamware, it included 1,282 different scenes. As Bentley, Wedgwood's partner, called for 'real views and real buildings' and sought 'the most embelished views, and the most beautiful Landskips, with Gothique ruins, Grecian temples and most Elegant Buildings', artists were sent scurrying throughout the country, laden down with camera obscura to ensure total accuracy.

The development which brought paintings into most homes at very little cost was aquatint, a method of tonal etching introduced by Paul Sandby in 1775. The process was simple yet effective, and professional engravers of aquatints became adept at faithfully reproducing the work of watercolour artists. A copper plate, dusted with fine particles of resin which, when the plate was heated, became minute globules of acid-resisting material, was 'bitten' with acid. The small cavities that held the printing ink gave an all-over tone. Following the outline drawing on the plate, which had already been deeply etched before the plate was dusted, the engraver, by a process of successive 'bitings' and 'stopping outs', in which the cavities were made either deep or shallow according to the length of etching time, obtained an accurate range of tones. The result was very like the Indian ink washes used as an underpainting by the early watercolourists, and ranged in tone from the palest of greys to a rich black. Highly skilled engravers were in great demand among publishers and artists alike. Though their fees were far from princely, at first £25 each plate, later £50, they were far higher than those of the artists. Turner, already famous, was paid at one time £7-10s for each drawing to be engraved; later this was

reluctantly raised to £10-10s. Though immediate returns were low, the engravings brought the artist's work to the attention of a far larger public, increasing the possibility of individual commissions (as well as satisfying personal ambition).

When hand-coloured with washes of transparent watercolour by a team of highly proficient women colourists, an aquatint print was deceptively like the original drawing. The superlative quality of the even washes led a later topographical artist, Samuel Prout, to write in 1813: 'It is not unlikely that the day may arrive when the connoisseur of a future age shall turn over the pages of a book, and pause upon an aquatint print, with the same solemn delight as those of our day are wont to do upon a woodcut of Albert Dürer, an etching of Hollar, or a production of any ancient engraver.' He was quite right!

Artists were sent all over the British Isles by print publishers until there was hardly a single stately home or ruined castle, cathedral or church, river or mountain that had not been recorded. Their meagre pay prevented artists travelling by carriage and most of them trudged from place to place on foot. They often travelled hundreds of miles, loaded down with the impedimenta of their trade (and more often than not uncertain of the night's lodging). Many of them reduced their materials and equipment to a bare minimum, but Samuel Palmer for one set out on his sketching tours equipped like an Alpine climber.

The work of the early topographers often shows a distinct charm, but it was so meticulous in detail as to seem overworked. Notable exceptions to this general trend were some of the lively pen and ink

Opposite: *Godington, Kent.* Michael 'Angelo' Rooker, 1746-1801. Watercolour over pencil (Victoria and Albert Museum, London)

Below: *Castle Point, York.* John Warwick Smith, 1749-1831. Never so strong as those of Towne, nevertheless Smith's watercolours received lavish praise in his day (Yale Center for British Art, New Haven)

Right: *Elvet Bridge, Durham.* Thomas Hearne (British Museum, London)

and watercolour studies of Anthony Devis and Thomas Hearne. Devis (1729–1817), born into a family of artists, was a competent draughtsman who worked in the tradition of the Dutch school of painting. His 'stained drawings' were made by overlaying slight tints, on outlines drawn either in black chalk or with a pen charged with watered-down Indian ink. John Alexander Gresse (1741–94) and Samuel Hieronymous Grimm (1733–94) were also instrumental in fostering the popularity of the 'stained drawing'. Grimm, born in Switzerland, was a much-travelled artist who was commissioned by Gilbert White to illustrate *The Natural History of Selbourne.* White wrote of him 'His price is two guineas and a half per week. His buildings, human figures, quadrupeds, waters, perspective among trees, are good; but his trees are not so pleasing: he has also a vein of humour, but that I shall not allow him to call forth, as all my plates must be serious.'

John Inigo Jones (1720–1810), another of the school of topographical artists, was a scene painter at Covent Garden. His *The Maid of the Mill*, engraved by William Woollett, became a great success and went a long way to help his election as a founder member of the Royal Academy. Numerous other artists working in watercolour added something, however small, to the growing movement, among them Moses Griffiths (1747–1809) and Willie Reveley (d1799). Slightly later, and more significant, were 'Warwick' Smith and Francis Towne.

Francis Towne (1739–1816) was said to have painted in oils from the age of fourteen and this remained his sole medium, apart from preliminary studies made in pen and wash, until 1777, when he began to take a greater interest in watercolour. His interest developed during a tour of Wales made in that year, from which he brought back a series of drawings in pen and wash that he later used as a basis for paintings in both oils and watercolour. It was in Wales that he first became aware of the grandeur and artistic possibilities of mountain scenery, which was to bear fruit later in his magnificent Alpine scenes.

Among the Alps in 1781 Towne blossomed out as a great watercolour painter. He was overawed by the towering peaks, ridges and glaciers, and his awareness of their crushing power comes over strongly in his paintings. Unlike most of his contemporaries, he made no attempt to soften the harsh contours of the scenery. The colour in his Alpine landscapes is restrained. Modulating blues, violets and greys with great skill, he concentrated mainly on tone, form and sweeping design to give his work strength. Towne made only his preliminary

Opposite: *Source of the Arveiron.* Francis Towne, 1740-1816. Watercolour over pen and ink. In this, probably his most famous watercolour, Towne conveys the crushing power of the Alps which so overawed him (Victoria and Albert Museum, London)

104

drawing on the spot. His pen line and tints were added in the studio

John 'Warwick' Smith (1749–1831) was a friend, admirer and rival of Towne. No one is certain why he was nicknamed 'Warwick'; some say because the Earl of Warwick was his patron, others because he settled in Warwick from about 1781. In the autumn of that year he travelled home from Italy through Switzerland in the company of Francis Towne, and like him made a number of studies which he later worked up as watercolour paintings. It is interesting to compare the work of these two artists, deriving from the same subject matter. Beside those of his friend, Smith's watercolours lack force; the colour, while clean and transparent, is hesitant, almost timid. His contemporaries, however, took a different view. They were lavish in their praise. 'No one, I believe ever came so near the tint of nature as Mr. John Smith', wrote Julius Caesar Ibbotson. Another fellow artist wrote, 'Smith was the first artist to unite depth and richness of colour.' Yet another, 'His most successful works, though not many in number, certainly surpassed in the union of light, shadow and colour, all that has been produced before.' His transparent colour, washed over either a pen or pencil outline, is pleasant and unassuming – grey-blues, with touches of bistre, red and dark green – but despite the laudatory remarks of his contemporaries, Smith's colour was never as effective as Towne's. For some reason Towne seems to have escaped the notice of the critics of his time.

A pupil of Towne, John White Abbott (1763–1851), of whom it was said, 'he practises as a surgeon, and only paints by snatches, though by choice he would always so be engaged', followed closely in the footsteps of his teacher. While working in the same flat, decorative washes of colour, reinforced with an even pen outline, his work lacks the inner conviction of Towne. John Baverstock Knight (1785–1859) was another who followed Francis Towne without quite achieving Towne's quality.

Among a slightly later group of topographic painters in watercolour, whose work had a decidedly architectural bent, were Theodosius Forrest (1728–84), Michael 'Angelo' Rooker (1743–1801), Edward Dayes (1763–1804), James Malton (1866–1803), who taught the young Turner, and Joseph Farington (*d* 1821) who, though no great artist himself, was a powerful figure in the art world of his day as well as a keen observer and recorder of the contemporary scene. Edward Dayes was the outstanding member of this group who were active toward the end of the 18th century. If for nothing else, Dayes will be remembered for the influence he had on the watercolour painting of Turner and Girtin.

Right: *Lympne Castle.* Edward Dayes, 1763-1804. (Laing Art Gallery, Newcastle upon Tyne)

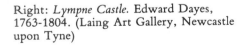

18

Thomas Girtin: Forging a Tradition

According to Laurence Binyon, Thomas Girtin (1775–1802) was 'one who, if we regard his relation at once to his predecessors and to his successors, seems even more than Turner in his dazzling isolation, the central figure of the whole watercolour school.' Many may disagree with that assessment; certainly, Girtin's work was surpassed by Constable and Turner, but he did point the way to the great Romantic artists that followed him. Towards the end of his short life, he formed a bridge between Italian Classical landscape and Dutch realism, between the topographical and the Romantic. These styles were never completely exclusive – there was indeed considerable overlapping – but by and large the watercolour artists of 18th-century England were drawn to one or the other.

The advent of pure watercolour – as opposed to tempera and fresco painting – as a phenomenon in the history of Western art, was confined to England and reached its heyday between 1775 and 1840. It was an important manifestation of the Romantic period provoked by the Industrial Revolution – the movement from an agrarian society towards an urban, industrial and commercial society, which was

Two views of Durham Cathedral by Thomas Girtin, 1775-1802. They clearly show his development as a watercolourist (below, Victoria and Albert Museum, London, and bottom, Whitworth Art Gallery, University of Manchester)

accompanied by a challenge to the existing social order voiced by Burke, Paine, Hume and others.

New ideas on the freedom of the individual were also manifest in the Romantic movement in the arts, which by the end of the 18th century was affecting landscape painting in watercolour. It was Girtin more than any other watercolourist who, although reared as a topographer, was the originator of the new Romantic attitude. One critic said of him, 'Not one characteristic watercolour of the early nineteenth century could be imagined without presupposing Girtin.' And, writing twenty years after the artist's death, William Henry Pyne, a founder member of the Society of Painters in Watercolour, fully appreciated Girtin's importance. 'Girtin was proceeding with the same observant eye to nature, and equally attentive to that captivating quality, local colour. These two aspiring geniuses [Girtin and Turner]

Kirkstall Abbey, Thomas Girtin. A watercolour painted about 1799 with added penwork over pencil underdrawing (Victoria and Albert Museum, London)

. . . were developing new properties in the material with which they wrought their elegant imitations of nature, and raising the practice of watercolours, which had hitherto procured no higher title for the best works of its professors, than tinted drawings, to the rank and character of painting in watercolours. . . Girtin prepared his drawings on the same principle which had hitherto been confined to painting in oil, namely, laying in the object upon his paper, with the local colour, and shadowing the same with the individual tint of its own shadow. Previous to the practice of Turner and Girtin, drawings were shadowed through, whatever their component parts . . . all with black or grey. It was this new practice, introduced by these distinguished artists, that acquired for designs in watercolours upon paper, the title of paintings.'

While it is generally true, as Pyne said, that most artists before

Eidometropolis – part of a panoramic view of London. Thomas Girtin (British Museum, London)

Girtin employed a monochrome underpainting method, and more often than not began with an outline, there were exceptions. Throughout the history of watercolour there has been an overlapping of attitudes and methods, and Towne, Taverner and Skelton, among others, often dispensed with underpainting and worked directly with local colour.

Very little is known for sure of Thomas Girtin's short life: he left no autobiographical material, and at the time of his death his painting had not made sufficient impact on the art circles of the day to merit the interest of a contemporary biographer. Legend grew up around his life as his work began to be appreciated and his significance in the watercolour movement was recognized. At face value, some of it appears true, but much remains doubtful.

It has been established that Girtin was born at Southwark, the son of a brushmaker or, according to some authorities, a rope and cordage contractor. Two months later, Joseph Mallord Turner was born over a barber's shop in Maiden Lane, the other side of the Thames. Girtin was first apprenticed to a drawing master named Fisher, but later became a pupil of Edward Dayes, an established topographical artist. Legend has it that their relationship was a stormy one, due to Dayes's jealousy of his pupil, but the only evidence is a note by John Pye, the engraver: 'Young Girtin, he tells me, soon excelled his master, which "this jealous & small-minded person" never forgave him. The praise bestowed on his pupil was gall to him & increased his hatred. In order to check his progress, he employed him to colour prints week after week & month after month.' When Girtin rebelled, the legend continues, Dayes had him committed to Bridewell as a refractory apprentice. This tale is not corroborated by records from Bridewell and seems highly unlikely. But that some friction existed between the two men there can be no doubt; Dayes ended a piece written after Girtin's death with the cruel remark, 'Girtin died . . . at the early age of twenty-seven years: but intemperance and irregularity have no claim to longevity.'

About the time he broke contact with Dayes, Girtin met James Moore, a wealthy city merchant with a taste for antiquities and the picturesque. Himself an amateur draughtsman of limited ability, he employed others to work up his sketches as illustrations for *Monastic Remains and Ancient Castles in England and Wales*. Moore probably introduced Girtin to the beauties of northern English landscape during one of his tours.

Two years later Girtin was attending Dr Thomas Monro's 'evenings' at the Adelphi. Monro was a royal physician and amateur painter who encouraged aspiring young artists. There, Girtin and Turner copied drawings by John Cozens and other friends of 'the good doctor', as Turner called him, grateful for the half-crowns and oysters provided. The two young men, so different in temperament, became good friends and made a number of sketching tours together – often making drawings of the same subjects – to produce topographical material for the growing commercial market.

Working alongside each other and equally impressed by Cozens, it was only natural that their paintings should develop along similar lines, but within a year or two they went their separate ways as independent artists. It is generally accepted that during his working life Girtin was the leader and Turner the follower. There is no doubt that Turner had a great respect for Girtin. Once when a dealer, after admiring his work, said that he had seen something finer, Turner replied, 'I don't know what that can be, unless it's Tom Girtin's *White House at Chelsea*.' Girtin was motivated on the one hand by a feeling of reverence for nature and a great respect for her beauty, on the other, by an urge to express, through nature, his own personal

Cayne Waterfall, North Wales. A brilliant almost effortless portrayal of cascading water by Thomas Girtin (British Museum, London)

Right: *The Market Place, Ross, Herefordshire*. Cornelius Varley, 1781-1873 (Victoria and Albert Museum, London)

feelings. Most of his early work falls into the topographical class, but in his last years – a lung infection killed him at twenty-seven – topography gave way to an emotional communion with the scene before him in a manner that links him directly to the Romantics who followed him.

John Varley (1778–1842), born three years after Girtin, was an enthusiast and a 'character'. One writer dismisses him as 'a facile systematizer. . . A number of his paintings at South Kensington bear witness to his deficiencies as a teacher.' This can hardly be true of a man who exerted so strong an influence on artists of the calibre of Cotman, Cox, de Wint, Linnell, William Hunt and Samuel Palmer.

Confident, commanding, humorous and abrasive, he was surely

Below: *Snowdon*. John Varley, 1778-1842 (Victoria and Albert Museum, London)

one of the most successful teachers of his time, with the happy gift of being able to pass on to others his own zest for life. He abhorred secrecy and unstintingly taught his pupils all he knew. He was equally generous in delivering his opinions to fellow artists; these were not always welcome, and there is more than a trace of venom in Constable's remark to a friend, 'Varley, the astrologer, has just called on me, and I have bought a little drawing of him. He told me how to "do landscape", and was so kind as to point out all my defects. The price of the drawing was a guinea and a half to a "gentleman", and a guinea to an "artist".'

Varley did indeed practise astrology, and anyone introduced to him for the first time would soon be asked their date and hour of birth, prior to a horoscope being cast. He became a constant companion of William Blake, and it was at his instigation that Blake drew his 'visionary heads' of historical characters – spiritual portraits that he could summon up at will. That Varley took Blake's visions as seriously as the mystic did himself cannot be doubted. He wrote on the back of *The Ghost of a Flea*, 'The Vision of the Spirit which inhabits the body of a Flea, and which appeared to the late Mr. Blake, the designer of the vignettes for Blair's *Graves* and the Book of Job. The vision first appeared to him in my presence, and afterwards till he had finished the picture . . . J. Varley.'

Although a consummate craftsman, producing watercolours outstanding in drawing, design and colour, Varley's chief claim to fame lies in the influence he had over other artists and the encouragement that he unselfishly gave to them. Varley too was taken up by Dr Monro who, judging by the powerful influence of Girtin on Varley's early work, must have recommended Girtin as the example for the young artist to follow. The work of his early period is carefully drawn and subdued in colour, with greys and blues especially owing much to Girtin; these characteristics Varley later passed on to Cox and de Wint. During his middle period he moved closer towards the Classical picture construction of Poussin and Claude and the *Liber Studiorum* of Turner (a series of prints inspired by Claude). As Varley said, 'Nature required cooking'. In his final period he became less effective, slipping into mannerism and forsaking careful observation for a slipshod artificiality based on his own curious interpretation of nature. He never achieved the inspired heights of his first idol, Girtin, nor that of his pupils, Cox and de Wint; nonetheless, John Varley's best watercolours are of high quality.

Mountainous Landscape: Afterglow. John Varley 1778-1842 (Victoria and Albert Museum, London)

19
Turner

A traveller by coach from Rome to Bologna in 1829 wrote, 'I have fortunately met with a good-tempered, funny, little, elderly gentleman, who will probably be my travelling companion throughout the journey. He is continually popping his head out of the window to sketch whatever strikes his fancy, and became quite angry because the conductor would not wait for him whilst he took a sunrise view of Macerata . . . From his conversation he is evidently "near kin to", if not absolutely, an artist. Probably you may know something of him. The name on his trunk is J.W. or J. M. Turner.'

Joseph Mallord William Turner (1775–1851) was obsessed by his art, driven to create by a force that he could hardly control. His passion for drawing led him to fill sketchbook after sketchbook: quick pencil studies made from rolling ship or jolting carriage, beautifully recorded ideas, or small watercolour gems of the places he visited. He could scarcely pass anything by without recording it.

Turner was the complete professional. Bound to his work by the dedication of genius, to him drawing was the embodiment of thinking. His output was prolific. No artist before or since has left such a complete documentation of his development, from his work as a student to his last great masterpieces. Each of the stoutly bound sketchbooks in which he usually made his notes was numbered and,

Norham Castle, Northumberland. Turner
(British Museum, London)

together with a brief description of its contents, stored away in his reference library. By the end of his life he had accumulated over 19,000 sheets of drawings, notes and watercolour sketches.

Turner was born near Covent Garden, London. From an early age he showed a precocious talent for drawing: the copies of prints and sketches from nature he made were hung up for sale in his father's barber's shop, priced between one and three shillings. Already the young boy was acutely aware of the value of money, a trait he shared with his father. They came to regard three things only as important: paintings, profits and privacy.

For a time the young Turner took lessons in perspective from Thomas Malton, an architectural draughtsman who advised his father to make him a tinker or cobbler as he showed no aptitude for topographic drawing. Nevertheless, his father entered him as a student at the Royal Academy schools when he was fourteen. By the age of fifteen he was exhibiting at the Royal Academy; at twenty-four he was elected an Associate and three years later became a full R.A. His work at this stage in his development, as in the watercolour *The Archbishop's Palace, Lambeth* (1790) is stiff and formal, owing much to his time with Malton. But by 1796, a work like *Interior of Ely Cathedral: Looking from the North Transept and Chancel*, one of several large watercolours he was painting at this time, was demonstrating his emerging genius. Viewed from well below eye level, it shows growing assurance in drawing and perspective – that plunging perspective so favoured by Girtin and himself. Turner's sketchbooks

115

Right: *View over the Roman Campagna.*
Turner (British Museum, London)

of this period show him moving towards new visual concepts: both his drawing and his manipulation of colour were becoming more skilful and there is evidence of that feeling for light that was so to obsess him in his later years.

Around 1794 Turner and Girtin were taken up by Dr Thomas Monro, in whose house in the Adelphi they copied old masters, 'two to a candle'. Both were strongly influenced by Cozens, learning from him to build up rich tones in a series of small brush strokes, layer upon layer. The two young men also went on sketching tours together, travelling on foot, twenty to thirty miles a day, their few possessions at the end of a stick. By 1802, the year of Girtin's tragic death, their styles had separated. Whereas Girtin was content to create beauty from the facts before him, Turner eagerly invented, imposing his own ideas upon the subject he was painting. At the time of his death, Girtin was probably the more proficient watercolour artist. No one was more aware of this than Turner, who wrote 'If poor Tom had lived, I would have starved.' Nevertheless, Turner was already a success, his work highly sought after. He bought a house in central London and set it up as a private gallery.

There are numerous stories about Turner's meanness; both he and his father were misers. The house in Queen Anne Street was allowed to fall into disrepair; paper peeled from the walls and one visitor wrote, 'The top of his gallery is one ruin of glass and patches of paper . . .' Potential collectors were offered a single glass of sherry from a broken decanter. His father, travelling from their second house at Twickenham to open the gallery, rode to town in a market gardener's cart seated on a pile of vegetables – for the price of a glass of gin.

Turner's use of oil paint affected his watercolour technique. By experiment he discovered that it was possible to build up a total scheme on paper working from dark to light. The study of *Norham Castle* is built up of thin, glazed washes of greens, pink, yellow and pale blue, here and there rubbed through to create a sense of light. The following contemporary description illustrates his methods:

Right: *Caernarvon Castle.* Turner (British Museum, London)

The lights are made out by drawing a pencil [brush] with water in it over the parts intended to be light and raising the colour so damped by means of blotting paper; after which with crumbs of bread the parts are cleared. Such colour as may afterwards be necessary may be passed over the different parts. A white chalk pencil [Gibraltar rock pencil] to sketch the forms that are to be light. A rich draggy appearance may be obtained by passing a camel Hair pencil 'nearly dry' over them, which only 'flirts' the damp on the part so touched and by blotting-paper the lights are only shown partially.

By 1827 Turner had reached the height of his success, although his greatest watercolours, his most ambitious excursions into the realm of 'flittering light', as he put it, were still to come. By that time he had travelled abroad to Switzerland, Germany, France and Italy.

Below: *Lonely Dell, Wharfedale.* Turner (Leeds Art Galleries)

Masterpieces, one after the other, flowed from his brush: *The Great Fall of the Reichenbach, Tivoli, Tobias and the Angel, Splugen Pass* and *The Rigi* (watercolours). Turner was fascinated by Mount Rigi, a jutting rock on the banks of Lake Lucerne, and made study after study of it, of which *The Rigi at Sunset* ('Red Rigi') and *The Rigi at Sunrise* ('Blue Rigi') are among his greatest masterpieces. These two pictures especially demonstrate Turner's mastery of the watercolour medium. He used every technique in his considerable repertoire to

Overleaf: *Rigi with Full Moon.* Turner was fascinated by Mount Rigi, a jutting rock on the banks of Lake Lucerne. This is only one of many studies he made of it (British Museum, London)

221

Right: *Venice, The Grand Canal with the Salute.* Painted in 1840, this is again Turner at his most ethereal (Ashmolean Museum, Oxford)

Right: *Vase of Lillies, Petworth.* One of Turner's remarkable flower studies painted during his stay at Petworth House, Sussex (British Museum, London)

produce shimmering iridescence – washing, blotting, rubbing, scraping and retouching, stippling and hatching. His *High Street, Oxford*, painted in the 1830s, is hardly more than scintillating light. All yellows, but for a hint of light mauve and blue, it has a group of barely delineated figures in the foreground while in the background a church, just discernible, peeps out pale against an already light sky: detail has given way entirely to atmosphere. *Venice: the Grand Canal with the Salute* (1840) displays all his mastery at capturing placid, still water: a vibrant sky and in the distance a building, the San Giorgio Maggiore, misty and insubstantial.

Turner's handling of light in his watercolours affected his approach to oil painting, much to the consternation of traditionally minded contemporaries. In his lifetime, Turner was not without his critics. A group of fellow watercolourists condemned 'the vicious practice of Turner and his followers', and the use made of reflected light by the Turner school caused some to dub them 'white painters'. But Turner also had his supporters, particularly John Ruskin (his most vigorous champion), John Martin and Francis and Thomas Danby.

Above: *On the Rhine* (Victoria and Albert Museum, London)

Right: *Holy Island, Northumberland, c.*1820s (Victoria and Albert Museum, London)

20

Constable

Turner was one of the few indisputably great English artists. As it happened, another great English artist was painting in watercolour at the same time. John Constable (1776–1837) painted watercolours chiefly for 'pleasure and remembrance' or as studies for future oils. During his lifetime that aspect of his work was little known and hardly affected contemporary developments in watercolour.

Unlike Turner, John Constable grew up a country boy, whose lasting love of the Suffolk countryside inspired many of his major works. As a successful landscape painter in London he wrote, 'The Londoners with all their ingenuity as artists, know nothing of a country life, the essence of landscape.' For Constable, landscape was everything. Country sights, sounds and country ways held a deep fascination for him even as a boy. The play of the sun on a still millpond, rich, flickering hedgerow shadows – 'I even love every stile and stump, and every lane in the village [East Bergholt], so deeply rooted are early impressions.'

Constable stood at the parting of the ways between his great predecessors, who presented landscape in terms of sweeping composition with only as much resemblance to nature as they saw fit, and his successors, who faithfully recorded nature at the expense of pictorial quality. Constable was the first to prove that a landscape could be a great work of art while remaining a faithful likeness of nature. Watching the sails of his father's mill turn against racing clouds, he became a master of skies, and recognized, in the words of Benjamin West, '. . . that light and shade never stand still . . . in your

A sketch inscribed 'Borrowdale 13 Oct 1806 – Afternoon'. This sketch begins to show the feeling for light that was to blossom in Constable's later work (Victoria and Albert Museum, London)

skies always aim at brightness.' Constable himself wrote: '. . . the sky is the keynote, the standard of scale, and the chief organ of sentiment . . . the sky is the source of light in nature, and governs everything.'

When John Constable was born on 11 June 1776, he was not expected to live through the night. Whatever the weakness was – there is no record – he grew into a healthy child and a strong, handsome young man. At school in Lavenham he suffered at the hands of a 'flogging usher'; later, he attended Dedham Grammar School, where he stayed until he was seventeen. It was there that he developed a taste for drawing and painting. His father, having failed to persuade him to take Holy Orders, wanted him to come into the mill with a view to taking it over on his retirement. But his son's heart was not in it. He had become friendly with John Dunsthorne, a local craftsman who taught him to paint from nature. Dunsthorne was an ingenious, naturally talented man, a plumber and glazier by trade who, as well as painting, played the flute and made musical instruments. He instilled in the young Constable a love of nature and, more important, taught him method. Together they would paint a particular view until the shadows changed, when they would pack up and go home, returning the following day at the same hour to continue their picture.

An amateur artist and collector from Dedham, Sir George Beaumont, impressed by Constable's ability and enthusiasm, advised

Watercolour and pencil sketch of clouds. 'The sky is the keynote, the standard of scale, and the chief organ of sentiment.' (Victoria and Albert Museum, London)

Above: *Trees, Sky and a Red House* (Victoria and Albert Museum, London)

sending him to London for advice and study. Reluctantly his father agreed, and in 1796, at the age of nineteen, he set off for London, where he stayed with an uncle and aunt at Edmonton. He met 'Antiquity' Smith, an engraver and drawing master, who counselled caution. He also met and worked with Joseph Farington R.A., no great artist but a man of perception, who at an early stage thought Constable's style of landscape would one day 'form a distinct feature in art'. Constable continued to paint, but two years later, when his prospects as an artist seemed as dim as ever, he wrote to Smith, 'I must now take your advice and attend to my father's business, as we are likely soon to lose an old servant (our clerk), who has been with us eighteen years; and now I see plainly it will be my lot to walk through life in a path contrary to that in which my inclination would lead me.' However, this dire fate was avoided. Two years later he became a student at the Royal Academy, exhibiting there for the first time in 1801. In 1819 he was made an Associate, finally becoming an R.A. in 1828.

Left: *Stoke-by-Nayland* (British Museum, London)

Overleaf: *Stonehenge.* One of his greatest works, this watercolour is a classic example of Constable's bold treatment of skies, an approach that was not fully appreciated until fifty years after his death (Victoria and Albert Museum, London)

127

1629 88

Seaport with a Storm Passing. Although he had little time for seascapes, those that Constable did paint are among the best of their kind (British Museum, London)

By that time Constable had long made his name as a landscape painter – he had also married and was raising a family – but his robust technique, his broad, massive treatment of his subject matter, was criticized by many of his contemporaries, including Ruskin, whose adulation of Turner seems to have blinded him to Constable's greatness. Sales came slowly and he often found himself in financial difficulties, but he still insisted 'there is room enough for a natural painter', i.e. one who attempts to portray, '. . . light, dew, breezes, bloom and freshness'. He added, 'the great vice of the present day is "bravura", an attempt to do something beyond the truth. Fashion always had, and will have, its day; but truth in all things will last, and can only have claims on posterity'. His view never changed, and although he rarely exhibited his watercolours and never his free sketches, these express even more than the finished oils his approach to nature and his art. In *Clouds*, a small watercolour sketch, 7½ in. × 9 in. (19 × 23 cm), the direct boldness of his approach is seen at its best. The carefully observed clouds flit across an easily suggested, watery blue sky; in the distance, giant cumuli build up with a faint tint of greyish mauve. Benjamin West's advice is again apposite: '. . . even in the darkest effects there should be brightness. Your darks should look like darks of silver, not of lead or slate.'

Constable's early watercolour notes of Derbyshire, made in 1801, were done in pencil and sepia, but by 1806 his *The Victory in the Battle of Trafalgar*, showed a masterly grasp of colour. Although

strongly influenced by Girtin, his highly individual talent was becoming apparent; his portrayal of natural lighting, his 'feel' for composition, as well as his handling of colour – all are evident in *A Bridge, Borrowdale*.

The years between 1828 to 1834 saw Constable at the height of his powers as a watercolour artist. In these years he painted *Stonehenge – Wilts*, *Old Sarum in a Storm*, possibly his most vivid watercolour study, full of sparkling life, *Stoke-by-Nayland* and innumerable sketches.

In his later watercolours such as *Landscape Study* and *Fittleworth Bridge and Mill, Sussex*, Constable drew with brush as well as pencil, applying his colour with vibrant, separate strokes rather than even washes. He often flicked out high lights with the wooden end of his brush or a penknife. His mature fluidity of style and broken forms were nevertheless carefully controlled; his sureness put Constable among the great watercolourists of all time.

Constable's legacy was perhaps more important in France than in England. The French Romantic painters, reacting against the mannered Neo-Classical art of David and the Revolution, and looking for artistic freedom as others looked for political freedom, eagerly welcomed the spontaneous but scrupulously accurate work of Constable. Meanwhile other painters were at work in the charming, undramatic countryside of East Anglia, though their watercolours had little direct connection either with Constable or the French Romantics.

21

The Norwich School

The Norwich Society was founded in 1803 (it is said) by John Crome (1768–1821) and Robert Ladbrooke (1770–1842), two young professional artists neither of whom had received much in the way of a formal education. The somewhat florid manifesto of the Society, prepared at the Hole in the Wall tavern in Norwich, suggests an anonymous driving force behind the idea. This might well have been Dr Rigby, a public-spirited professional man of some local importance. The stated purpose of the Society, was 'to conduct an Enquiry into the Rise, Progress and Present State of Painting, Architecture, and Sculpture with a view to point out the Best Methods of Study to attain Greater Perfection in these Arts', and it must be more than a coincidence that its rules were the same as those of the Speculative Society, which met at the same tavern and whose principal was Dr Rigby. This same doctor had employed John Crome as an errand boy in his surgery.

The Norwich Society was most active between 1805, when the members held their first exhibition, and 1833; but it was not created out of a vacuum, nor did it come to a sudden end. Broadly speaking, the lifespan of what is now known as the Norwich school began when Crome finished his apprenticeship and continued to the death of Joseph John Cotman in 1878. The city of Norwich has a history of patronage dating back to the Middle Ages, when it was the second-largest city in England (except perhaps Bristol), and there were many capable artists living in the area at the beginning of the 19th century. While the more memorable works of the Norwich school – by 1828, 328 artists had exhibited at the Norwich Society exhibitions – were based on East Anglian scenes, it was never narrowly provincial. Its members were open to the influences of other English watercolourists working within the framework of the Romantic revival. The effect of the French wars on continental travel, coupled with a growing delight

Right: *Mountain Scene, Patterdale.* John Crome (Fitzwilliam Museum, Cambridge)

Opposite: *Wood Scene,* 1810. John Crome, 1768-1821 (Victoria and Albert Museum, London)

Palings and Tree by a Pond. John Crome
(British Museum, London)

among artists such as Richard Wilson and Gainsborough in their native land, caused patrons who had previously demanded scenic paintings of Italy and the Alps to clamour for British scenes.

The Norwich school, perhaps surprisingly, was the only significant group of provincial artists to form themselves into a society. Though Crome and others often painted in oils, the greater part of the work of the Norwich school was executed in watercolour and, apart from a few oils, these represent their most significant contribution to early 19th-century art. The patriotism that fired the English gentry to turn to native artists applied in a provincial way to East Anglia, where the wealthy burghers of Norwich were the chief patrons of the Norwich school. With this in mind, the Society once used a quotation of Sir Martin Shee, president of the Royal Academy, at the head of their exhibition catalogue to the effect that pictures should be bought from the 'heart' – meaning through motives of loyalty – rather than 'taste'.

In the generation before the founding of the Norwich Society, a number of Norwich painters had already gained a national reputation, but most of them had gravitated to the capital where, despite fierce and ever-growing competition, the rewards were greater. Among them were John Ninham (1754–1817), who produced a number of topographical pieces in the 'stained-drawing' tradition; James Sillett (1764–1840), an architectural draughtsman; the Cattons, father and son; Capon (1757–1827) and Joseph Brown (1720–1801), who was known as the 'Norwich Claude'. A perhaps more original artist was William Williams, known as Williams of Norwich (*fl* 1770–92). Relatively few of his watercolours remain, but they have a charm that is more than the conventional Romanticism of his day.

Despite this substantial body of Norwich-bred painters, it was left to local men, John Crome and his brother-in-law Robert Ladbrooke, to lay the foundations of the Norwich school.

Seldom has a great artist, and Crome was a great artist, been so modest, so reluctant to display his talents, yet this retiring, shadowy figure was the driving force behind a significant art movement that added a considerable chapter to the history of watercolour. 'Old Crome' – as he became known to distinguish him from his son 'Young' (John Bernay) Crome – was born at the Griffin, an inn kept

by his father in Norwich. Possibly it was not a thriving alehouse, as Crome senior was also a journeyman weaver. Apart from occasionally visiting London and making one or two tours of the Lake District, Crome spent his whole life in Norwich, drawing his subject matter from the surrounding countryside. Only once did he go abroad: at the age of forty-six he paid a brief visit to Paris to see the Italian sculpture and paintings amassed by Napoleon, which were on exhibition.

After rudimentary schooling, he went along with other Norwich youngsters to 'the Palace', an open space in the city frequented by young people in search of work. It was there that Dr Rigby chose him to be his errand boy, and for the next two years he delivered medicine to the doctor's patients. Seeking a better job he became apprenticed to a sign painter, who taught him the mysteries of colour mixing and

Right: *The Ferry House, Pull's Ferry, Norwich.*
James Stark, 1794-1859 (Castle Museum,
Norwich)

Below: *Interior of a Barn.* Miles Edmund
Cotman, 1810-1858 (Castle Museum,
Norwich)

brush control. He also met Robert Ladbrooke, his future brother-in-law, a printer's apprentice with whom he shared an attic studio. Here at night the two young men would copy and colour prints – much as Turner and Girtin were to do at Dr Monro's in London – teaching themselves drawing by trial and error. From the end of his apprenticeship in 1790 until 1803, when the Society was founded, he scratched a living by painting inn signs, giving drawing lessons to the daughters of the local gentry and selling an occasional picture. He had meanwhile married a local girl and in 1801, when he was thirty-three, he was appointed drawing master to Norwich Grammar School.

As a painter, Crome was not surprisingly a slow developer. He was twenty-two before he finished his apprenticeship; at the same age Cotman, Varley and Girtin became famous. It was the paintings owned by a local collector, Thomas Harvey, which really triggered off the genius of Crome, particularly those of Wilson and the 17th-century Dutch picturesque landscape painter, Hobbema. They were to exercise a deep and lasting influence on him throughout this life: his last words were allegedly, 'Hobbema, my dear Hobbema, how I loved you.' Crome, together with Wilson and Girtin, forms a link between the picturesque tradition and the Romantic revival.

Crome's watercolours were painted as studies or for his own pleasure; they are full of an intense personal feeling. Never a mere topographer, he chose his subjects for the paintings he could make of them, not for their historical or architectural interest. He maintained that 'trifles in nature must be overlooked that we may have our feelings raised by seeing the whole picture at a glance, not knowing how or why we are so charmed.'

His first watercolours (the earliest survival is *The Mill Wheel*) were traditional in technique, with local colour washed over grey monochrome, but by the time the Norwich Society was formed his work had broadened into direct and honest interpretation of things seen: this was to be the hallmark of Crome's work.

A feature of the Norwich school was the difficulty many of its members had in handling figures, which were often ill-drawn, mannered and unreal. This is certainly true of John Thirkettle (1777–1839) and Robert Ladbrooke. Thirkettle, although 'arranging' his pictures more than Crome, who tended to record a segment of nature, was rarely just picturesque, and with his delicate, subtle colour, never sentimental. Robert Dixon (1780–1815), a theatrical scene painter, and

Charles Hodgson were original members of the Norwich Society who exhibited in 1805. With Crome, Thirkettle and Ladbrooke they were the mainstay of the early exhibitions. Later they were joined by Joseph Stannard (1797–1859), known mainly as a painter of seascapes, and John Stark (1794–1859), a pupil of Crome.

Another of Crome's pupils, the Rev. Edward Thomas Daniell (1804–43), was one of the more adventurous members of the school. He was a wealthy amateur to whom art was all-important, more perhaps than the Church, and in 1841 he resigned his living to join a survey party on the ship *Beacon*, bound for Greece. His dashing watercolours made in Greece and the Middle East caused one critic to write, 'these sketches drawn on half sheets of buff-toned paper, loosely outlined with a hardish pencil; the local colours indicated with somewhat sloppy washes of sepia, ultramarine, brown pink and gamboge; the details enforced with a reed pen, in bistre and burnt sienna, and sometimes heightened with white, are always satisfactory and sometimes very charming indeed.'

Among other important younger members were Robert Leman (1799–1863), whose watercolours, executed in creams, a pale straw, delicate blues, a hint of green and light mauves, have a precision of line and sense of spaciousness, Thomas Lound (1802–61) and Henry Bright (1810–73), an artist with a strongly individual style. One of the last members of the Norwich School was John Middleton (1827–56) whose short career produced pure watercolours of great beauty. He had a gift for capturing the emotion of a scene; a feeling for the vitality, sensations and memories of the countryside which he passes on to the viewer. His glimpses of nature are recorded in rich, authentic colour.

The Norwich school was a group of artists sharing a love of their native East Anglia, who worked honestly and unselfconsciously to produce watercolours which often 'charm we know not why'. But, besides Crome, John Sell Cotman, who joined the Society in 1807, went far beyond the rest and became one of the great watercolour artists of all time.

Dock Leaves. John Middleton, 1827-1856 (Castle Museum, Norwich)

22

John Sell Cotman

Opposite: *Drop Gate, Duncombe Park*. John Sell Cotman, 1782-1842. One of the greatest technicians, Cotman saw nature as a challenge, to be analysed and ordered (British Museum, London)

'Let him rather black boots than follow the profession of an artist.' John Opie, the fashionable London portrait painter, visiting Norwich in 1798, thought little of sixteen-year-old John Sell Cotman's chances, and said so in his usual blunt way. (Opie was given to bluntness: asked by a Norwich enthusiast how he mixed his colours, he replied, 'With brains, Sir.') However, notwithstanding Opie's advice, Cotman set off for London to 'learn to be a painter' that same year. In the event, the famous man's assessment of Cotman was in part true, for he did 'skulk through life as a drawing master and pattern drawer to young ladies.' Opie, however, was guilty of a major blunder, which time alone has rectified. Nowadays John Sell Cotman (1782–1842) is regarded as one of the leading figures in the history of watercolour.

When Cotman returned to Norwich in 1807, he joined Crome as a leading member of the Norwich Society. But the two men were quite different in both character and artistic outlook. Crome, untutored, placid and companionable, accepted nature as it was and recorded its spirit. Cotman, temperamental, given to fits of extreme melancholia, saw nature as a challenge, to be analysed and ordered. Landscape and sea have no limits, but a picture is bound by its frame; Cotman arranged and ordered the elements of nature within his paintings into a preconceived pattern. He sought by his own brand of pictorial logic to reveal to the viewer the secrets of nature as he saw them. His sensibility and absolute sincerity of purpose are the progenitors of that tender, lyrical quality characteristic of Cotman's work.

Cotman was born in Norwich in 1782, but very little is known of his family background – not even his father's profession. At any rate, his father had sufficient faith in his artistic talents to send him off to London in the face of Opie's advice. The young Cotman found employment on Ackermann's magazine, *The Repository of Arts* for which he coloured prints and generally made himself useful. He soon

Below: *The Needles*, painted *c.*1823. This study, using a simple range of colours, has all the qualities of a Japanese woodblock print (Castle Museum, Norwich)

Shady Pool. J. S. Cotman (National Galleries of Scotland, Edinburgh)

came to the notice of Dr Monro, and it was probably at 'the good doctor's' house that he first met Girtin and Turner. His meeting with Girtin had a powerful effect not only on the two artists themselves but on the subsequent direction of English watercolour. Some of Cotman's early drawings are indistinguishable from those of Girtin, but he soon began to assert his own unique approach to composition, which in turn influenced Girtin.

Cozens, Girtin and others, had imparted romantic feeling to their pictures while retaining topographical accuracy. Cotman went further; he consciously designed the natural elements within his paintings to achieve a balance between the picturesque and the Classical.

In June 1800, at the age of eighteen, Cotman was awarded a prize by the Society of Arts for his watercolour *A Mill*; the same year he exhibited six other paintings at the Royal Academy. 'Conspicuously on his side', wrote one commentator, '. . . is his sense of actual drawing or painting as a thing of artistic and emotional value in its colour, line and massing over and above, or at best, through and through, the significance of the objects represented.'

During his first Welsh sketching trip, made later the same year, the originality of Cotman's approach to landscape paintings became more clearly apparent. Although still influenced by Girtin, he was beginning to build up his pictures in broad planes, one behind the other, rather like a stage set; the mountains, trees, rivers and rocks were arranged to create an aesthetic pattern on the paper. Already he was eliminating inessentials, resolving his trees into bold masses and shapes, his mountains and rocks into tonal planes.

While acclaimed by his fellow artists, Cotman was still forced to eke out a living by making copies for a printseller and giving drawing lessons. In advance of one of his periodical returns to Norwich, he inserted an advertisement in the Norwich *Mercury*: Mr Cotman informs his friends that during his stay in Norwich, which will be from three weeks to a month, he proposes giving lessons in drawing to those ladies and gentlemen who may think his sketching from Nature or style of colouring beneficial to their improvement. Terms: Half a guinea an hour.' After Girtin's death in 1802, Cotman was recognized by the young artists of the Brothers, a sketching society formed for the study of Romantic landscape, as the leader of contemporary watercolour.

Greta Bridge, 1805. J. S. Cotman (British Museum, London)

The Dismasted Brig. Although less than sympathetic towards marine subjects, Cotman was able to convey wind and water brilliantly (British Museum, London)

Fortune smiled on Cotman when he became drawing master to the family of Francis Cholmeley of Brandsby Hall, fifteen miles north of York. He became a firm favourite with the whole Cholmeley family, to whom he was known as 'dear Cottey', and acquired more patrons among the Yorkshire gentry. The paintings he produced between 1803 and 1805 represent his work at its best; according to him it was the time of 'the real inspiration for the full development of [his] art'. He never again reached the same heights, just as Samuel Palmer, the Romantic visonary, never equalled in quality the watercolours made during his Shoreham period. Between these years Cotman painted *Brecon Bridge*, *The Drop Gate* and probably his greatest masterpiece, his first *Greta Bridge* (the later version painted in 1810 lacks the spontaneity of the original).

Cotman applied his colour directly, one tint upon another, but only when the first was dry or nearly dry (unlike de Wint, for instance, who deliberately ran one colour into another). In consequence his washes are precise shapes without blurring at the edges. Often he applied a second wash of the same tint to achieve an added richness of colour. In many ways his watercolours are reminiscent of Japanese wood-block colour prints, and it was only after these had appeared in Europe during the 1860s that Cotman's work came to be fully appreciated. Yet it is certain he never saw a Japanese print. He painted in the studio, working from detailed, searching, pencil drawings made on the spot: 'emotion recollected in tranquility', as Wordsworth put it.

Soon after his marriage in 1809 Cotman, with a family to support, remembered Francis Cholmeley's advice that 'every artist must, to a degree, obey his master the public' and attempted to produce work with more commercial appeal. From this time onwards his life was one long struggle to earn enough to support himself and his family. His pictures were slow to sell: while he tempted the public with romantic and historical subjects, he could not bring himself to abandon his decorative yet objective style. This, coupled with the fact that watercolour was still the poor relation of oil painting (Joseph Wright of Derby voiced a general opinion when referring to watercolour as 'an amusement for young ladies') put Cotman under severe financial and mental strain.

The brilliant promise of his early days never brought Cotman the success and appreciation he merited; that was to come from later generations of art lovers. He became a manic depressive, who alternated between periods of unbounded optimism and fits of hopeless melancholy. 'My views in life,' he wrote, 'are so completely blasted that I sink under the repeated and constant exertion of body and mind. Every effort has been tried, even without hope of success. Hence the loss of spirits amounting almost to despair. . . My amiable and deserving wife bears her part with fortitude – but the worm is there. My children cannot but feel the contagion.' The new year of 1842 saw him feverishly painting, collapsing, and painting again. He died in July, 'of discouragement – of a broken heart'.

John Sell Cotman's sons, Miles Edmund (1810–58) and Joseph John (1814–78), met with no more material success than their father before them. Miles Edmund made a meagre living as a teacher. Joseph John committed himself to painting in a highly individual range of colour. In *River Landscape*, for example, rich golds and lemon yellows vibrate against vivid blues and Indian reds, anticipating the emancipation of colour that was to come much later. He too had little material success with his pictures. Like his father, he slipped into moods of acute depression and when he died, destitute, a friend had to pay for his coffin.

*Chirk Aquaduct, c.*1803-04. J. S. Cotman (Victoria and Albert Museum, London)

143

23

David Cox and Peter de Wint

Watermill in North Wales. David Cox, 1783-1859. From his very first visit Cox became fascinated by North Wales, returning to it time and again (Victoria and Albert Museum, London)

'How fond you are of painting wind, Mr. Cox.' The lady who said that to David Cox (1783–1859) may have had penetrating insight or may have been babbling vacuously. At any rate, Cox took it as the highest compliment.

A year younger than John Sell Cotman, he was a very different character from that sad, tormented genius. Cox was a stable, ruddy-faced, genial man, whom Turner nicknamed 'Farmer' Cox. He worked diligently at the business of becoming a painter. In his earlier days he was fired with a reforming zeal that drew him towards the teachings of Joseph Hume. Once, as a protest at the high tax on tea, he concocted his own beverage, which consisted of a brew of new-mown hay. He and his unfortunate family drank it for a time but eventually Cox had to capitulate to the iniquitous revenue, doubtless through family pressure. Though generally placid, he could be provoked into a sudden fit of temper. As a newly wed husband desperately trying to earn a living, he turned to Euclid for the secrets of measured perspective but, failing totally to understand the diagrams, he hurled the book through the flimsy wall of his home.

Cox also differed from Cotman in his approach to watercolour. Cotman, despite his volatile nature, brought to his work a calm serenity, filling his pictures with mature trees, mellow farm buildings and churches. Cox sought to catch the movement and underlying spirit of nature in all her capricious moods: the movement he could see in racing clouds, whirling kites, spinning windmill sails, or the wind tugging at a skirt on an open beach. He worked rapidly across the paper, setting down almost instinctively what he saw that was fascinating in nature, and the outcome was no less revealing than the more considered vision of John Sell Cotman.

Cox was stirred by such great artists as Constable and Turner, who at the time of Cox's development were painting some of the finest landscapes ever produced. It was said, 'no artist appreciated Turner's genius more than Cox did.' Yet, deeply moved though he was by Turner's work, Cox did not allow its influence to dominate his own talent; at an early stage he began to develop an individual style that would eventually secure him a place among the great exponents of watercolour. Cotman had shown great promise as a youth, but Cox had to struggle to achieve, first competence, then brilliance. Even in old age, when he was producing his most eloquent and, to the modern eye, most appealing work, its quality depended largely on the artist's interest and involvement in the subject. His simple, almost naive character, his fortitude and industrious application, are not always apparent in his seemingly effortless wash drawings. Nevertheless, these qualities are the governing factors in his most successful watercolours.

David Cox was born in Deritend, one of the poorer quarters of Birmingham. A rather delicate boy, he was the son of a smith who forged gun barrels, bayonets, horseshoes and the like, and grew up among the flying sparks and acrid smoke of forges and the clangour of family metalwork shops. An accident as a schoolboy was the unlikely reason for his initial interest in art. Tripping over a door scraper, he broke a leg and was confined to the house for some time. During this enforced idleness a cousin gave him a box of paints. Immediately fascinated by colour, he passed the time daubing the kites that his school friends brought to him to decorate.

On leaving school, he followed his father's trade. The engraver John Pye later noted, 'When I first knew David Cox he was employed to wield the great hammer at a blacksmith's shop in Windmill yard.' A

145

On Lancaster Sands. David Cox achieved a remarkable sense of space using only a limited palette (Yale Center for British Art, New Haven)

short trial convinced his father that the lad would never make a blacksmith and, after a period at a drawing school, in 1798 he went as an apprentice to a toymaker, who put the boy to painting miniature pictures on snuff boxes, lockets, buckles, and buttons. His master's suicide brought his apprenticeship to an abrupt end, and the seventeen-year-old joined the Birmingham Theatre, grinding colours

and washing brushes for the scene painters. In the evenings he took
drawing lessons at a school run by the artist Joseph Barber.

When his chief, James de Maria – Cox always referred to him as
an artist of considerable talent – left the theatre, Cox took his place
touring with the company, and often played bit parts himself. After a
quarrel with Macready, the owner, he joined the famous Astley's

Circus, which took him to London. In 1808 he married his landlady's daughter, Mary Ragg, and they set up home in a small cottage on the edge of Dulwich Common, then a wild place frequented by gypsies and tinkers, whose donkeys, caravans and picturesque clothes formed the subjects of the young artist's early compositions. Mary, twelve years his senior, proved a good wife who, until her death in 1845, showed great sympathy for her husband's ambitions, wholeheartedly encouraging him when his confidence flagged. At that time things were tight for the young couple and Cox was forced to supplement his income by painting '310 yards of scenery at 4s per square yard'.

Before his marriage he had taken drawing lessons from John Varley who, though only five years older, was already one of the most successful teachers of his day. That kindly man not only taught him the basic rudiments of traditional watercolour, of which he was a master, but, once he learned that Cox was an aspiring artist, taught him for nothing. Cox, in line with the practice of the Romantic watercolourists of the day, made a sketching tour in Wales, where the scenery so captivated him that he returned time and time again, becoming a well-known figure at the Royal Oak in the village of Bettws-y-Coed. Until 1813, when he took a post at the Military Academy at Farnham (with the courtesy rank of captain) Cox supported his family by giving drawing lessons, taking chance scene-painting commissions and now and again selling a watercolour. The average price was one guinea each; on 30 November 1811, he noted that he had sold a dozen for eight shillings each. In 1814 he took up an appointment at Miss Croucher's school for young ladies in the city of Hereford, where the family remained for thirteen years.

At Hereford Cox came to the full realization that light, shade and colour could and should express personal emotion. He developed a completely individual style using broken colour, applied with short, swift brush strokes, to create the effect of changing light and atmosphere.

By the time he returned to London in 1827 Cox had some reputation in the world of art, but his drawings still fetched only small prices. His account book for 5 July 1830 shows: 'Five watercolour drawings, viz., Calais Pier, View in Ghent, Boat in the Scheldt near Dort, Minehead, and a landscape in Wales – price for the five, £12'. Not until 1836 was there any sustained demand for his work, and then

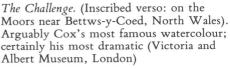

The Challenge. (Inscribed verso: on the Moors near Bettws-y-Coed, North Wales). Arguably Cox's most famous watercolour; certainly his most dramatic (Victoria and Albert Museum, London)

only for smaller pictures which sold for five or six pounds. In 1836 he discovered the absorbent Scottish wrapping paper, whose soft, grey, flecked surface added such character to his later work.

In 1840 Cox left London for good to settle down in Harborne, in those days a rural village two miles outside Birmingham. 'London,' he said 'is quite Babylon; the WHIRLING of carriages quite bewilders me and makes me giddy.' At Harborne he entered his third and most successful period as an artist. For the next fifteen years, until his sight failed, he painted with all the recaptured vigour of youth. Stripping his work of drawing-master dexterity, he painted with a simplicity and sincerity that reflected his own forthright character. Watercolour masterpieces flowed effortlessly from his brush; *Rhyl Sands*, described by the critic Roger Fry as 'right outside the conventions of his day and prophetic of a quite modern outlook', *Flying the Kite*, *The Frightened Flock*, and the greatest of them all, *The Challenge*. When totally absorbed in his subject David Cox reached the height of greatness, for as he remarked, 'Merely to paint is not enough, for when no interest is felt nothing is more natural than that none should be conveyed'.

Born at Stone in Staffordshire a year after David Cox, Peter de Wint (1784–1849) worked for John Raphael Smith, the London engraver, following in the footsteps of Girtin and Turner who also in their youth coloured prints for Smith. De Wint, descended from an old family of wealthy Amsterdam merchants, was a highly religious man. Each morning before breakfast he either learned a text by heart or wrote a prayer. He was a prickly character given to fits of irritability and ill temper, a man to be treated with caution, who despite his short temper, lived an uneventful life of domestic happiness. He taught his pupils with sincere understanding and threw himself wholeheartedly into his annual sketching tours. 'I do so love painting,' he once said, 'I am never so happy as when looking at Nature. Mine is a beautiful profession.'

His subject was almost exclusively the English scene – his one visit to Normandy left him unimpressed – and he was happiest painting cathedrals and castles high above still rivers, mellow russet brick cottages, haystacks and lush pastures, weather-worn churches and sailing barges on still waters.

De Wint's work has a calm serenity. He delighted in reflections in still water; not for him the whirling vortexes of Turner's storm-tossed seascapes. His rich, beautifully balanced colour was obtained from a severely limited palette of Indian red, vermilion, purple lake, yellow

Above: *Lincoln.* Peter de Wint. Using only two brushes, both large, one pointed, the other stubby, de Wint was able to achieve either a fineness of detail or a sweeping bold wash (British Museum, London)

Right: *By the Wayside.* Peter de Wint (Yale Center for British Art, New Haven)

ochre, gamboge, brown-pink, burnt sienna, sepia, Prussian blue and indigo. Occasionally he introduced touches of orange ochre, Vandyke brown, olive green and emerald. He restricted himself to the use of two brushes only, both large, one finely pointed, the other stubby and well worn. With these he was able to achieve the fineness of detail of his *Lincoln* or the sweeping broad treatment of *The Wayside.* He often used a sharp penknife to flick out highlights, and for this reason, if no other, used a thick, rough-surfaced paper, Old Creswick or Whatman. He developed the knack of keeping light passages wet, then running in rich, fuller colour, imparting a luminosity to his darker tones that could not be obtained by superimposing two or three colours one upon the other.

Ruskin who was blind to the greatness of Constable, fully appreciated the genius of David Cox and Peter de Wint. 'Suppose,' he wrote, 'that we had nothing to show in modern art, of the region of the raincloud, but the dash of Cox, the blot of de Wint, or even the ordinary stormy skies of our inferior watercolour painters, we might yet laugh all efforts of the old masters to utter scorn.'

24

The Visionaries

'. . . Spirit and vision are not, as the modern philosphers suppose, a cloudy vapour or a nothing; they are organized and minutely articulated beyond all that mortal and perishable nature can produce. He who does not imagine in stronger and better lineaments and in stronger and better light than his perishing and mortal eye can see, does not imagine at all. . . Men think they can copy nature as correctly as I copy imagination. They will find this impossible.'

Contemporary with Turner, Constable, Cox and de Wint were a group of visionary artists who used watercolour to express an imagery beyond that of the human eye. William Blake (1757–1827), and to a

Wise and Foolish Virgins. William Blake, 1757-1827. 'Men think they can copy nature as correctly as I copy imagination. They will find this impossible.' (Fitzwilliam Museum, Cambridge)

An illustration for *Songs of Innocence and Experience,* 1789. It was this style of drawing that so influenced the young Samuel Palmer (British Museum, London)

lesser degree Henry Fuseli (1741–1825), communicated a personal, inner message, and they influenced a number of younger artists, including Calvert, Varley, Flaxman, Linnell and Samuel Palmer, who called themselves 'the Ancients', and in some ways anticipated the Pre-Raphaelite Brotherhood.

Blake was the most imaginative artist of his or most other times. He was hardly recognized in his day, and as late as 1913 C. E. Hughes wrote in his *Early English Water-colour,* '[Blake's] paintings cannot be regarded as essentially a part of the English school of watercolour.' Today his genius is universally acknowledged and his influence on recent generations of British artists has been enormous.

William Blake's father, who ran a small hosiery business in Soho, London, was a dissenter addicted to Swedenborg. When he was four, Blake insisted that he saw God's head at the window, and at the age of eight he had a vision of the prophet Ezekiel and 'a tree filled with angels, bright angelic wings bespangling every bow like stars'. Only the intervention of his mother saved him a thrashing for lying from his sternly religious father. Since then the question has frequently been

Elohim Creating Adam. William Blake. Strong imagery and mysticism combine with a sensitive use of colour (Tate Gallery, London)

asked, 'Was Blake mad, or was he a true visionary?' Many of his contemporaries certainly thought him insane. Leigh Hunt, writing in *The Examiner* in 1809, referred to him as, 'an unfortunate lunatic whose personal inoffensiveness secures him from confinement.' To others, like Thomas Butts who bought a number of his paintings, John Linnell, George Richmond, John Flaxman and Samuel Palmer, Blake's visions were genuine. A solid, down-to-earth businessman, John Giles, referred to him as 'the divine Blake, who has seen God, sir, and talked with angels.' To Blake himself his visions were simple and natural, but he never tried to impose them on others. 'I am not ashamed, afraid or adverse to tell you what Ought to be told: That I am under the direction of Messengers from Heaven, Daily and Nightly. . . I never obtrude such things on others unless question'd and then I never disguise the truth.'

As a boy, Blake visited the studio of the eminent and popular William Ryland, engraver to the king, to discuss the possibility of an apprenticeship. On leaving he turned to his father and said, 'I don't like the man's face; he looks as if he would live to be hanged.' Twelve

Above: *The Spiritual Form of Nelson Guiding Leviathan.* Blake claimed he could summon up mystical images at will (Tate Gallery, London)

years later this respected artist was indeed hanged, for forgery.

William Blake was a lonely, dreamy child. His parents thought him too delicate to be sent to school, but they encouraged his drawing, giving him money to buy prints to copy. At the age of ten he took lessons at a drawing school and at fourteen he was apprenticed to James Basire, an engraver. The young Blake began to collect prints, showing a preference for the work of Raphael and Michelangelo. Throughout his life, the drawings of Michelangelo were his greatest inspiration, and their influence on his work is obvious to the most casual observer (though Blake never studied any of Michelangelo's drawings and paintings at first hand). The massively muscular figures of Michelangelo, together with a love of the Gothic fostered by the engravings he made of churches in Basire's workshop, mingled to fire the imagination of the romantic and sensitive boy.

At twenty-one Blake left Basire and for a time attended the Academy schools, exhibiting there in 1780. For the next seven years he earned a precarious living as an engraver for booksellers while writing poetry and composing watercolour drawings. In 1782 he married Catherine Boucher, a woman who was to stand by him all his life, staunchly supporting him during his recurring fits of depression. Some believe she helped Blake retain his sanity. Later he wrote:

'Madman' I have been called: Fool they call thee.
I wonder which they Envy – Thee or Me?

He set up as printseller and engraver in partnership with a former fellow apprentice, John Parker; but they were not successful and in 1807 the partnership was dissolved. By now Blake's poetry had become vital to him, and to accompany a major poetical work, *Songs of Innocence*, he had prepared a set of watercolour drawings. But lack of funds prevented publication. Day and night he struggled with the problem of how to publish, until one night, his dead brother Robert, appearing to him in a vision, showed him how it could be done. The following morning, Kate was sent out with all the money they possessed – half-a-crown – to buy the necessary materials.

The method of reproduction revealed to him by his brother was the forerunner of letterpress printing from acid-etched relief plates. The intaglio process of etching – the ink being drawn up and printed from an acid-etched line on a copper plate – had been in use for many years, but no one had thought to reverse the process. Drawing both his design and writing on a copper plate, probably using acid-resisting stopping-out varnish applied with a fine brush, he etched away the background with acid, leaving the image in relief. He rolled the raised surface with printing ink in any colour he required (his text was usually printed in red) and being careful not to allow it to touch the bitten parts of the plate, took a print in the manner of a woodcut. To these line prints he applied watercolour in iridescent washes of flaming red, limpid blues and subtle greens.

Samuel Palmer described the printed drawings for *The Marriage of Heaven and Hell* as 'marvels of colouring; such tender harmonies of delicate greens, and blues, and rosy pinks; such brilliancy of strong golden and silver lights; such gorgeous depths of purples and reds; such pictures of the dark chasms of the nethermost pit, lit up and made lurid by unearthly glare of flame tongues – it has been in the power of no mortal brain to fancy, and no mortal hand to depict.' Blake's wife said simply, 'Whoever will not have them will be ignorant fools and not deserve to live.'

Blake valued independence above wealth and though many patrons and friends set out to help him, he always ended up shying away in panic from the 'yoke of their polite patronage'. In 1795 someone procured for him the offer of the post of tutor in drawing to the royal

Opposite: *Jacob's Ladder.* William Blake (British Museum, London)

154

Satan Smiting Job. William Blake. The influence of Michelangelo is particularly obvious in this illustration (Tate Gallery, London)

family, but seeing a threat to his freedom of thought, he turned it down.

The post of royal drawing master would certainly not have suited a man who illustrated the writings of Mary Wollstonecraft, a man who was so delighted by the ideals of the French Revolution that he wore the red 'cap of liberty' and wrote *The Song of Liberty* and *The French Revolution*. He was never rich, he was never really successful; but his unbounded passion for painting and writing drove him to prepare countless illustrations, printed paintings and watercolours. When he was sixty, he was again reduced to hack engraving for publishers.

At times Blake showed symptoms of paranoia and depression, though close friends bore witness to his gaiety and lack of pretension. He seems only to have become obscure when refuting critics like the man who described the descriptive catalogue to Blake's unsuccessful exhibition of 1809 as 'a farrago of nonsense, unintelligibility, and egregious vanity, the wild effusions of a distempered brain'.

156

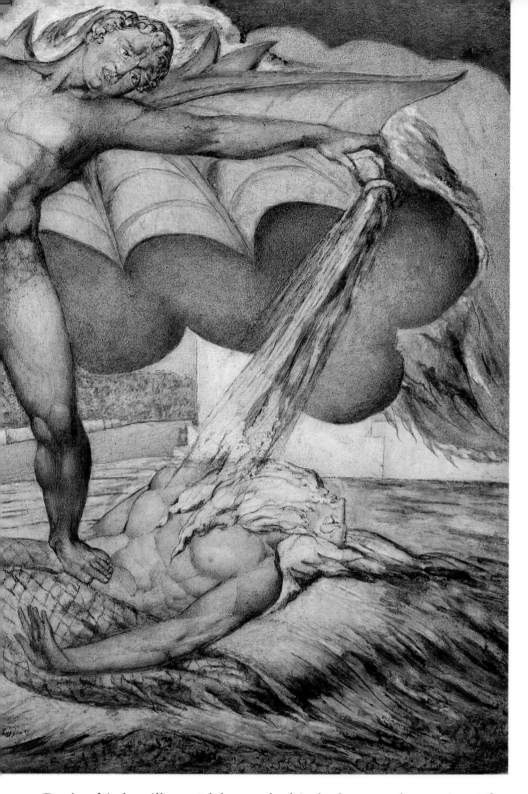

During his last illness Blake worked in bed on a colour print, *The Ancient of Days*, started many years before. Towards the end he said to his wife, 'Kate, you have been a good wife: I will draw your portrait.' He did so for an hour, then, laying down the drawing, he sang 'Hallelujahs and songs of joy and triumph', until death came.

Blake was an artist of great power, at times reaching heights that put him amongst the world's great imaginative artists. His mood could change from evangelical fire and fury, to tender, softly coloured, almost pastoral delicacy. He scorned technique, pushing media to the limits of their capacity and beyond; in consequence, many of his paintings, particularly his so-called tempera works, have changed in appearance and in some cases partly perished. He worked in line, delineating each form as a clear visual statement. Artists who failed to work in this manner he regarded as liars, hired by Satan 'to depress art'. Blake's approach to colour was abstract; he used it solely to express emotion, never to imitate naturalistic colouring.

Blake's contemporary and friend, Henry Fuseli (originally Füssli,
1741–1825) was born in Zurich. Through his friendship with Laveter,
a mystic with his own concept of Christianity and author of a famous
work on physiognomy, he was forced to leave Switzerland: it was said
that he and Laveter had attempted to conjure up the deceased lover of
a young Zurich girl. Despite his remark that Blake was 'damned good
to steal from', Fuseli always championed his cause as well as offering
personal help. In England he prospered from the very beginning, and
became a professor of painting and keeper of the Royal Academy. A
talented poet and orator as well as a painter, he was unable to
crystalize these talents to reach true greatness. Blake, who thought
Fuseli a hundred years ahead of his time, appreciated his friendship.
He scribbled fondly in his pocket book:

> The only man that e'er I knew
> Who did not make me almost spue
> Was Fuseli: he was both Turk and Jew –
> And so, dear Christian Friends, how do you do?

Fuseli's drawings and watercolours, violent and fantastic, dealing with
Gothic superstition, mythology and the world of the mind, appear
somewhat forced alongside Blake's renderings of profound conviction.

25

Samuel Palmer's Visions of the Soul

Early 19th-century English landscape painters were enthralled by nature's moods and changing seasons, which they faithfully painted, each as he saw them. Their Romanticism manifested itself with little or no contrivance in their work. Only the spiritual and prophetic revelation of William Blake came near the more consciously Romantic work of the contemporary German landscape painters such as Caspar David Friedrich (1774–1840) and Blake did no more than a handful of pastoral drawings. Nevertheless, the spiritual revelations of Blake had a profound effect on a few young admirers.

In 1819 Blake had produced 232 small wood engravings to illustrate Robert Thornton's version of Virgil's pastoral poems, and although Thornton himself was horrified at the result, Samuel Palmer and his companions were immensely stimulated.

Samuel Palmer (1805–81) the son of a Newington bookseller who was a strict Baptist, grew up among books and manifested a natural feeling for religion (both his grandfather and great-grandfather had been clergymen of some note). His nurse, Mary Ward, an unusual young woman who read Milton and the Bible to her charge, made a deep impression on Palmer. One night she and her charge stood

Tintern Abbey. Samuel Palmer, 1805-1881
(Victoria and Albert Museum, London)

Above: *Shady Quiet*. Samuel Palmer (Royal Society of Watercolour Painters, London)

watching a full moon over an elm. The golden serenity of the moon, the dense shadows of the foliage flitting along the wall, completely overawed the small boy. Quietly, Mary Ward recited a couplet to him.

Fond man! the vision of a moment made.
Dream of a dream, and shadow of a shade.

Samuel Palmer was never to forget this incident. Visions, dreams, shadows – though with light breaking through – were to become the dominant theme of his paintings.

Unlike most boys, this delicate, sensitive child spent a 'sedentary and precociously grave childhood', encouraged by his father to learn Latin at an early age and to plunge into English literature. He turned naturally to poetry and began drawing. By the age of twelve he had 'a passionate love for the traditions and monuments of the Church; its cloistered abbeys, cathedrals and minsters, which I was always imagining and trying to draw; spoiling much good paper with pencils, crayons and watercolours.' In 1819, aged fourteen, he exhibited three landscapes at the Royal Academy, the official seal of competence in art circles. It was about this time that he first saw the work of Turner, whose Italian landscapes and such watercolours as *A Rocky Pool with Heron and Kingfisher* had a marked effect on the young artist.

Soon after this, 'It pleased God to send me Mr Linnell as a good angel from Heaven to pluck me from the pit of modern art.' Later he was to be less sanguine toward the man whom one contemporary described as an 'eccentric, ruthless, quarrelsome, talented and detested artist . . . who developed into a suspicious, tyrannical, cruel egotist.' Yet, when John Linnell (1792–1882) met Blake in 1818, he took engraving lessons from him and helped the ageing mystic in many

Right: *The Villa d'Este*. Samuel Palmer. Although a fine watercolour, this lacks the sensitive, pastoral quality of *Shady Quiet* (Victoria and Albert Museum, London)

160

Above: *The Magic Apple Tree.* This is Palmer at his richest. During his stay at Shoreham he produced his most significant work, full of romance and mystery (Fitzwilliam Museum, Cambridge)

Left: *Moonlight, a landscape with sheep.* After his meeting with Blake, Palmer produced six sepia drawings of incredible intensity (Tate Gallery, London)

Right: *In a Shoreham Garden.* Watercolour and gouache (Victoria and Albert Museum, London)

other ways, not least by making it clear that he believed him a great artist and did not think him mad.

Linnell taught Palmer to study the work of Dürer and Lucas van Leyden and later did him a greater service by introducing him to Blake. The tremendous excitement of that first meeting is apparent in Palmer's words. 'On Saturday, 9th October, 1824, Mr Linnell called and went with me to Mr Blake. We found him lame in bed, of a scalded foot (or leg). There, not inactive, though sixty-seven years old, but hard-working on a bed covered with books [he sat] like one of the Antique patriarchs, or a dying Michel Angelo. . . And there, first with fearfulness, did I show him some of my essays in designs: and the sweet encouragement he gave me . . . made me work harder and better that afternoon and night.'

In Blake's pastoral engravings – 'visions of little dells, and nooks, and corners of Paradise . . . a mystic and dreamy glimmer as penetrates and kindles the inmost soul' – Palmer saw a world transformed; a world close to his own mystical dreams. Like Blake, he

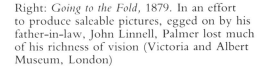

Right: *Going to the Fold,* 1879. In an effort to produce saleable pictures, egged on by his father-in-law, John Linnell, Palmer lost much of his richness of vision (Victoria and Albert Museum, London)

162

was fascinated by the written word; he filled his sketchbooks as much with written notes as drawings; short, staccato bursts, often changing to capitals and still larger capitals to stress a point: 'Why do I wish for a NEW STYLE? 1st, To save time. 2nd, To govern all by broad powerful, chiaroscuro. 3rd, TO ABOLISH ALL NIGGLE.'

The result of his contact with Blake was a series of six sepia drawings accompanied by quotations from Milton and the Bible. Some are intense moonlit landscapes: 'the rising moon seems to stand tiptoe on a green hill-top to see if the day be gone and if the time for her vice-regency is come.' In *Moonlight Landscape with Sheep*, a huge crescent moon blazes between dark, round trees, bathing both shepherd and sheep in lurid light and shade. *Early Morning* shows even more strongly Palmer's growing pastoral vision of a world of magic, where rabbits hop unconcerned through an idealized, densely textured landscape, where people sit beneath a monumental mushroom tree, and a thatched fairy cottage peeps above a waving sea of plenty.

Palmer became a member of the group of young artists calling themselves 'the Ancients'. Others were George Richmond, Edward Calvert, Francis Oliver Finch and H. Walter. Fired by the Nazarenes, a group of German artists who, in the manner of the Pre-Raphaelites, sought a return to the art of the late Middle Ages and set up a commune in the disused Roman monastery of San Isidoro, they too turned to the ancient poets and painters for inspiration. The Ancients settled in Shoreham, Kent, to dream their dreams, seeing nature not through the supernatural eyes of Blake, but as idealized, motionless, pastoral landscape. Palmer suffered from ill health and in 1826 he too, accompanied by his father and the faithful Mary Ward, moved to Shoreham, 'that genuine village where I mused away some of my best years'. During the seven years he lived at Shoreham Palmer produced his masterpieces, works of extraordinary imagination and beauty. His small, intense, pastoral scenes were, needless to say, not universally admired. 'What the Hanging Committee means by hanging these pictures without the painter to explain them,' wrote a critic of one exhibition, 'is past conjecture.'

Unlike Blake, Palmer would never have said that 'nature put him out'. On the contrary, he stayed close to nature, making copious sketches of the countryside, while still maintaining, 'I will, God help me, never be a naturalist by profession.' While at Shoreham, 'painting the visions of the soul', Palmer began to treat colour as an equal element of composition. Working in a mixture of watercolour, tempera, pen and varnish, he created works whose colour glows like stained-glass windows. The directness of his approach, his arbitrary use of colour and texture seems very modern, and influenced the work of Graham Sutherland and John Piper, among contemporary artists. He saw the whole of nature, leaf, fruit and blossom, as a 'conflagration of colour'; a Palmer sunset like *Orange Twilight* makes the rich, shadowed hills seem almost black.

His health recovered, Palmer moved back to London in 1833 to be near his friend Calvert. Four years later, at the age of thirty-two, he married Hannah, the eldest daughter of John Linnell. The couple spent the following two years in Italy, for Palmer a 'golden and glittering' land where 'you can only look at dazzling palaces, blazing in Italian sunshine, with your eyes half shut.' Back in England, Palmer was unfortunately dominated by his autocratic father-in-law, now a highly successful painter in oils, who continually urged him to paint in a more popular and therefore more profitable manner. As a result, Palmer's work completely lost the visionary excitement of the Shoreham days. His colour became merely garish, his composition conventional.

Above: *Harvest Moon* (Tate Gallery, London)

Left: *Bright Cloud* (Tate Gallery, London)

Palmer's great friend Edward Calvert (1799–1883), six years his senior, was born near Bideford in Devon, the son of a naval officer. He entered the navy himself but retired in 1820 to take up art as a career. During his time as a student at the Royal Academy schools, Fuseli, the keeper, introduced him to Blake. Like Palmer, Calvert was attracted by Blake's Christian mysticism, but he often turned to Greek mythology for his own subject matter. Palmer referred to his friend's 'naughty disobedient heresies', and by 1834 he was writing that Calvert was 'in deliberate hostility to the gospel of Christ'. It was whispered that he held sacrificial ceremonies in the garden at an altar dedicated to the god Pan!

One of the most striking qualities of Edward Calvert was his manual dexterity. His wood engraving *The Chamber Idyll*, which provoked Palmer's outburst, although no more than 1½ × 2½ in. (38 × 64 mm) is a wealth of complex detail. His watercolour *The Primitive City*, 3 × 4 in. (76 × 102 mm), is another of the jewel-like creations Calvert made with pen and wash. This quality of Calvert's influenced Palmer even more than Blake did, and it was to appear a generation later in the work of the Pre-Raphaelite, Rossetti.

26

Satire and Social Comment

Opposite top: *Vauxhall Gardens.* Although the colour has faded, this *tableau de mode* demonstrates Rowlandson's keen observation and quiet sense of fun (Victoria and Albert Museum, London)

Below: *The English Review.* Thomas Rowlandson, 1756-1827. A true satirist, Rowlandson saw funny incidents wherever he looked, but he was rarely cruel. (Copyright reserved. Reproduced by gracious permission of Her Majesty Queen Elizabeth II)

The medium of watercolour has often been used by satirical artists and caricaturists to comment on the life around them, either as finished paintings or as studies for works in other media. In many instances these studies formed the basis for hand-coloured engravings or etchings for a mass market. The social caricaturist drew attention to the follies of his time by exaggerating, sometimes in a good-natured manner, public and private idiosyncrasies. To Thomas Rowlandson (1756–1827), the sight of a coach being overturned on a bridge, the passengers flung over the parapet into the river, was cause for mirth, not for sympathy or anxiety. Like so many of his fellow satirical artists, he had a sharp eye for the ridiculous, and the ability to squeeze the maximum out of it visually. Others, less genial than Rowlandson, were scarcely comic at all, and their social or political comments expressed repugnance for real or imagined injustices.

When he died in 1827, Rowlandson was described in a contemporary obituary as a 'graphic humourist', but he and several of his fellow satirists were far more than that. They were accomplished watercolourists by any standard. Because they directed their artistic talents to subjects other than Romantic landscape, they are rarely included, or at best dismissed with scant reference, in many books dealing with the history of watercolour painting. Yet their watercolours have a sureness of draughtsmanship, brilliance of design and, in the case of Rowlandson at least, a delicacy of colour that compare with the work of more serious watercolourists of the age.

Rowlandson stands somewhere between the 18th-century French

commentators on fashionable society and the later, more radical work of Honoré Daumier (1808–79) and others. His father, a well-to-do tradesman, encouraged his son's talent as a draughtsman and allowed him as a student of sixteen to live with a widowed aunt in Paris. Here, for two years, he worked at the Ecole de l'Académie Royale, familiarizing himself with the paintings, drawings and gouaches of Fragonard, Baudouin, Lavrience and Vien. Although influenced by the vigour and brilliance of the French *tableaux des modes* his natural genius for humorous drawing began to assert itself.

When he was nineteen he returned to England and re-entered the Royal Academy schools, where his nude studies gained him the silver medal of the Academy in 1777. However, life did not run smoothly. About this time his father lost all his money in foolhardy speculation. The French aunt came to the rescue eventually; when she died she left young Rowlandson her fortune. Unfortunately, following in his father's footsteps, he became a regular habitué of the London gaming houses, where he soon lost his fortune. One contemporary remarked that Rowlandson 'frequently played through a night and the next day . . . such was his infatuation for the dice, he continued at the gaming table nearly thirty-six hours, with the intervention only of the time for refreshment.' Forced to earn a living, he turned to his reed pen (once, holding it up to a friend, he remarked, 'I have played the fool, but here is my resource') and at the age of twenty-six he threw himself into a series of watercolours which were reproduced as prints.

Rowlandson's comments on social abuses were never as astringent as those of Hogarth or Gillray; he was far happier recording the humorous side of the teeming life of London. But there was usually a barb in his pictures; naval officers taking rum with drabs aboard ship and tea with more ladylike females ashore; a well-fed man of the cloth receiving a pig as tithe from an undernourished farm labourer.

At the same time as he was producing his series of popular prints

Below: *A Windy Day*. Robert Dighton, 1752-1814 (Victoria and Albert Museum, London)

for Ackermann, he was trying to attract attention by producing ambitious *tableaux des modes: Vauxhall Gardens*, a watercolour exhibited at the Royal Academy in 1784, marked the beginning of his real success. This elegant painting, now unfortunately slightly faded in colour, is full of captivating detail with, on close examination, a wealth of comic expression and incidents. In the foreground of this picture of London's most fashionable pleasure gardens Rowlandson included a number of portraits of the leading society beauties and their beaux. Mrs Weichser, 'vocalist', sings from the balcony, Captain Topham, a famous dandy, blatantly quizzes the beautiful Duchess of Devonshire and Lady Bessborough; the one-eyed, wooden-legged Admiral Paisley is slightly more discreet in his attention. It was this large watercolour (19 × 29½ in. or 48 × 75 cm) more than any other that influenced his French contemporaries.

Vauxhall Gardens was followed in 1786 by *The English Review* and its companion piece *The French Review*, Rowlandson's largest and most ambitious watercolours (each 19¾ × 35 in. or 50 × 89 cm). The composition of *The English Review* as a whole lacks balance, with most of the action concentrated in the left-hand half of the picture. The massing of figures (often piled up in comical situations), the rearing and plunging horses, and most of all Rowlandson's ideal of female beauty bear witness to his admiration for Rubens. His friend Henry Angelo, in an obituary written for the *Gentleman's Magazine*, asserted that some of his drawings would have 'done honour' to Rubens. In his *Englishman in Paris*, Rowlandson clearly intends the three nubile dancers in a plush Parisian bordello being quizzed by a corpulent John Bull figure as a direct parody of the figures in the *Judgment of Paris* painted by both Rubens and Raphael.

Often unashamedly coarse, Rowlandson is never less than witty. Supremely indifferent to the changes in watercolour technique going on around him, he continued to follow the style of earlier painters in the medium. His draughtsmanship is crisp and clear, and his pale, attractive colours, applied with a full brush, transparent and flat, follow the confines of the pen or pencil; modelling and form are achieved by underlying monochrome washes. He normally drew with black or dark brown ink, introducing vermilion as a point of colour from the late 1790s onward. At the same time he modified his penwork to a thinner, more expressive line. His drawings intended for engraving and hand tinting were usually carried out in primary colours as far as possible, to simplify the work of the print publisher's

assistants. In watercolours not intended for engraving, his colour,
though light, is subtle and varied. To the end he remained a
draughtsman who employed colour to enhance an effect.

Henry Bunbury (1750–1811), one of the caricaturists working at the
same time as Rowlandson, was very popular in his day, but his
watercolour portraits were slight, and his sentimental book
illustrations lack the content of Rowlandson and the satiric bite of
James Gillray (1757–1815). Born the year after Rowlandson, Gillray in
the main produced scathing, and to modern eyes libellous, political
cartoons, which were engraved and hand-tinted with transparent
watercolour. Having neither the subtlety nor humour of Rowlandson,
his caricatures of the royal family and contemporary politicians are
overdrawn and usually bloated and grotesque.

Robert Dighton (1752–1814) was a curious character; a man of
many parts, watercolourist, actor, writer, singer and collector, he
eventually turned thief, smuggling Rembrandt etchings out of the
Print Room at the British Museum concealed in his own folio of
prints. He is perhaps best known for his political cartoons of the
Westminster Election – his caricatures were more charitable than
Gillray's – and a highly worked-up watercolour, *A Windy Day*.
Another artist of the time, George Cruikshank (1792–1878) used
watercolour mainly in the original sketches for his illustrations to
Charles Dickens's novels; but his *Ring of Fairies Dancing beneath a
Cresent Moon* shows a charming and sensitive use of watercolour.

27

The Pre-Raphaelite Brotherhood

Opposite top: *Excavations around The Sphinx.* Thomas Seddon. Painted in 1854, this strange watercolour with its almost photographic imagery is a triumph of technique (Ashmolean Museum, Oxford)

Opposite below: *Lucretia Borgia.* Dante Gabriel Rossetti (Tate Gallery, London)

Below: *Arthur's Tomb.* Dante Gabriel Rossetti, 1828-1882. Rossetti was totally absorbed in medievalism and *Arthur's Tomb* expresses a deep personal experience (Tate Gallery, London)

The Pre-Raphaelite Brotherhood began as a movement to revitalize painting and became an aesthetic movement that questioned the fundamentals of Victorian culture. Far outrunning the intentions of the young men who founded it, the movement became concerned with the role of the creative individual in an increasingly industrial and mechanical society (those 'dark satanic mills' so hated by William Blake) that created drudgery and bred slums. In many ways the movement echoed the sentiments of the Nazarenes, the group of German Catholic artists who influenced Palmer and his friends, though it was less expressly religious. The Pre-Raphaelites associated themselves with what they considered to be the ideals of the 15th century. Taking the masters of the Quattrocento as their inspiration, they set out to regenerate British painting by adopting Ruskin's doctrine of 'truth to nature' and seeking what they saw as the simple, truthful art of the early Renaissance. To a painstakingly accurate realism they added meaning and morality.

In the 1840s an artist like Daniel Maclise (1810–70), who painted ponderous historical scenes and drew facile portraits of literary figures, could be described as 'out and away the greatest artist that ever lived'. Some young students at the Royal Academy schools were disenchanted with the melodramatic chiaroscuro, the gesturing poses, hollow emotion and loose brushwork of so much contemporary art and sought a style of 'absolute independence as to art dogma and convention'. A book of engravings by Carlo Lasino, after the frescoes of Benozzo Gozzoli (1420–98), was one catalyst which led to their

admiration of the painters who came 'before Raphael'. In 1848 Dante Gabriel Rossetti (1828–82), John Everett Millais (1829–96) and William Holman Hunt (1827–1910), together with four others, founded the Pre-Raphaelite Brotherhood which, they agreed, should stand for 'absolute and uncompromising truth in all that it does, obtained by working everything, down to the most minute detail, from nature, and from nature alone'. Violently opposed to the aesthetic concepts contained in the *Discourses on Art* of Sir Joshua Reynolds (1723–92), the great panjandrum of English art in his time but known to them as 'Sir Sloshua' – they adopted a precise outline of form, brilliant colour, even light and passionate, minute observation of detail. Rossetti in particular was attracted by Blake's 'wiry line of rectitude', which the outspoken mystic recommended against the formless 'filth' of Rembrandt, Rubens and Reynolds. For their subject matter they turned to medieval romance, sharply seen sunlit landscapes, biblical scenes and pictures with a pronounced moral message. John Ruskin, seeing a danger of sentimentality in their preoccupations, wrote, 'If their sympathies with the early artists lead them into mediaevalism or Romanism, they will of course come to nothing.'

The first works of the Pre-Raphaelite Brotherhood were shown in 1849 by Millais and Holman Hunt at the Royal Academy and by Rossetti at the Free Exhibition, (an event held annually just prior to the Royal Academy exhibition). They were well received and all three paintings sold. People wondered at the initials PRB, inscribed after the artists' signatures, but the formation of the Brotherhood was still a secret. The following year, when their aims became public knowledge, they were flayed by the critics and spurned by the public. Holman Hunt (whose work was described as uncouth) and Millais ('plainly revolting') were undeterred by this or by Charles Dickens's review of Millais's *Christ in the House of his Parents*, which described Mary as 'a kneeling woman so hideous in her ugliness, that (supposing it were possible for any human creature to exist for a moment with that dislocated throat) she would stand out from the rest of the company as a Monster, in the vilest cabaret in France, or the lowest gin shop in England.' Rossetti, however, was hit hard by such invective, and he began to drift away from the ideals of the PRB into his own world of medieval decoration.

Rossetti was brought up in a family well read in Italian literature – his father was a Dante scholar as well as a dabbler in Italian revolutionary politics – and at an early age he began to identify himself romantically with his medieval namesake. Until the formation of the Brotherhood in 1848, he was still undecided whether to take up art or literature as a career. His affinity for the late medieval period was sincere and passionate, uncontaminated by the cloying nostalgia of some other Pre-Raphaelite paintings of medieval subjects. Well aware of his technical shortcoming in draughtsmanship and perspective, he thought in terms of two-dimensional designs in which colour was the vehicle of emotion. He wrote, 'to obtain some knowledge of colour', to Ford Madox Brown (1821–93) who, though never a member of the PRB, became closely associated with the movement later. Both he and Holman Hunt advised Rossetti to concentrate on still life, but this discipline was not to the liking of Rossetti. He decided to learn from his own mistakes, and *Ecce Ancilla Domini*, painted in 1849–50, clearly shows his continuing struggle with perspective.

The beautiful Elizabeth Siddal became Rossetti's 'Beatrice' and subsequently his wife, and in the years before her death in 1862 (from an overdose of laudanum) he produced a series of jewel-like gouaches based on the Arthurian legends. *Arthur's Tomb* expresses a deep personal experience; Rossetti's total involvement in medievalism is symbolized in its intensity of emotion, design and colour. His *Sir Galahad at the Ruined Chapel*, glows like a stained-glass window. In his memorial painting for his wife, *Guggum*, made shortly after her death, Rossetti came close to identifying himself with Dante grieving over the death of Beatrice. From then on, although he fell in love with Mrs William Morris and made painting after painting of her, his work lost much of its intense emotional force. He slipped into self-indulgence and his medievalism became an affectation. He was aware of this himself when he wrote, 'Look in my face, my name is Might-have-been; I am also called No-more, Too-late, Farewell.'

The Mill on the Thames at Mapledurham. George Price Boyce (Fitzwilliam Museum, Cambridge)

Some other Pre-Raphaelites produced watercolours, notably John Brett, George Price Boyce and Thomas Seddon, as well as Ford Madox Brown. Sir Edward Burne-Jones (1833–98) began as a close

follower of Rossetti, though he later moved towards a more personal style. Revolting against the growth of industrialism around him, he found refuge in medievalism as a means of escape – a medieval dreamworld with none of the fervour and honesty of Rossetti. *The Arming of Perseus*, a painting in tempera of 1877, is a fair example of his Greco-Gothic wonderland, while also showing charming deployment of restrained colour and elegant form.

Merlin and Nimeau. Sir Edward Burne-Jones, 1833-1896 (Victoria and Albert Museum, London)

28

Explorers' Art

Watercolour, mechanically so much easier to handle than oils, was the obvious choice of medium for artist explorers intent on recording the flora and fauna of newly discovered lands. Not only did water dry far more quickly than oil, but the amount of equipment required was minimal – a few cakes of colour, three or four brushes, pens, pencils, a handful of chalks and a supply of paper. Armed only with this primitive equipment, the artist explorers, and often explorers who

Indian Chief c.1585. John White, active 1570-1593. One of the earliest explorer-artists, White brought back to England with him a number of finely observed watercolours (British Museum, London)

The manner of their attire and painting them selues when they goe to their generall huntings or at theire Solemne feasts.

The broyling of their fish ouer the flame of fier. 11^b

Left: *Cooking fish.* John White (British Museum, London)

were not artists, made watercolour records which in many instances are works of outstanding beauty. Sometimes drawn quickly, on the spot, they have a freshness and spontaneity that transmits the wonder and awe of the artist to the viewer.

Wherever explorers went, they recorded their experiences, though since the invention of photography watercolour has inevitably declined as a means of communicating the scene in jungle, desert or glacier.

The explorers of the ancient world have left little evidence of their travels, apart from a number of Egyptian frescoes depicting the people of 'Punt'. In the watercolour and gouache illustrations to the 14th-century manuscripts of Marco Polo's account of his travels, the people of Asia and their buildings look deceptively European.

In the 16th century, when the maritime countries of Europe were sailing to the four corners of the world in search of new lands, Spanish and Portuguese expeditions took with them artists to make records of the people they had seen and the natural life of the territories they had discovered. Some of the work of the explorer artists was sketchy, and some was romanticized for the benefit of the folk at home. Indians and Africans were still depicted as dark-skinned Europeans, but by the 18th century, when the great Pacific voyages and scientific expeditions were beginning, the general standard was commendably accurate.

Unfortunately, few of the early drawings have survived and we have to rely on the explorers' written accounts of the wonders they encountered on their travels. For example, in the 1570s Francisco Hernandez, physician to Philip II of Spain, assembled a team of artists

Below: *View from Funchal.* William Hodges, 1744-1747 (National Maritime Museum, London)

175

and observers to produce a systematic record of the life of the people of Mexico, the country's resources and its flora and fauna. Together, the coloured drawings and notes filled fifteen manuscript books, but sadly they were all destroyed by fire in the late 17th century. Jacques Le Moyne de Morgues, who went with a French Huguenot expedition to Florida in 1584, was commissioned to make drawings of 'anything new', but these were lost when the Spanish overran the colony, massacring most of the French. Le Moyne, among the few to escape, left his watercolours behind, but he later made a curious painting, *Young Daughter of the Picts*, showing a naked girl painted from head to foot with flowers, many of them unknown in Europe at that time.

John White, an artist of real talent, who made contact with Le Moyne in England, accompanied Sir Richard Grenville's fleet of 1585, which sailed to found an English colony sponsored by Sir Walter Raleigh in North America. During the year he spent in Virginia he made countless drawings and watercolours of Indian life, birds, fishes, reptiles and plants; he also surveyed and mapped the areas explored by the colonists. His album of drawings is entitled in his own handwriting: 'The pictures of sondry things collected and counterfeited according to the truth in the voyage made by Sr Walter Raleigh knight/ for the discovery of La Virginea. In the 27th yeare/ of the most happy reigne of our soveraigne lady Queen/ Elizabeth and in the yeare of O^r/ Lorde God./ 1585'. It is the most complete graphic account of the time.

The artists who accompanied the conquistadors left vivid if not very faithful watercolours of the life and customs of the Aztec and Inca civilizations, depicting the customs and dress of the people and usually portraying them in a bad light (no doubt to justify the cruelty inflicted upon them by the conquistadors themselves). Many of the watercolours of Indian sacrifices are graphic and disturbing. Less

Little Ki Island, one of the watercolour illustrations from Lieutenant Pelham Aldrich's journal (Royal Geographical Society, London)

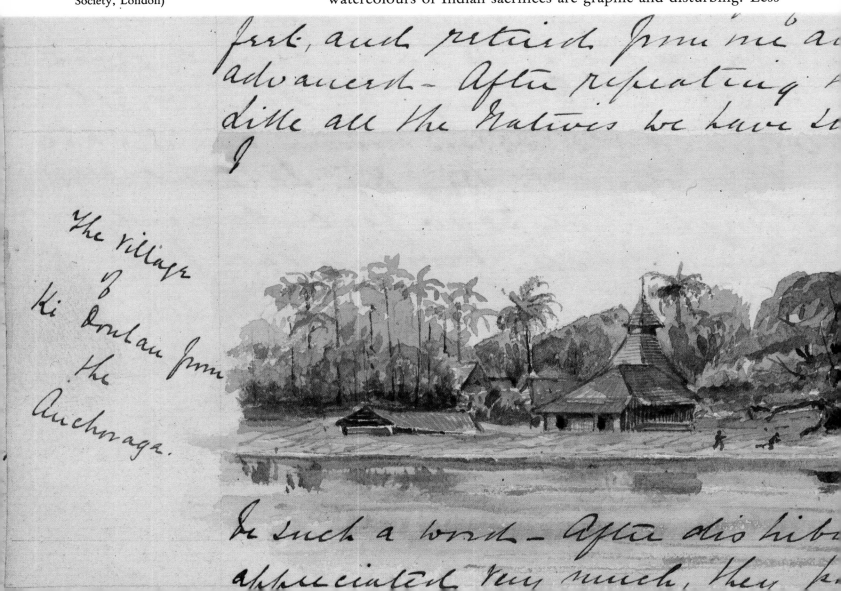

bloodthirsty and certainly more artistically acceptable, are a series of early hand-coloured engravings of life on the island of Hispaniola. In these, the artist has made an attempt to record accurately the life of the Indians. One drawing in this series shows sugar being refined on a plantation, with each part of the process faithfully observed.

The 17th century provides more informative work by the artist explorers, notably during the short-lived Dutch possession of Brazil. The first governor, Count Maurits of Nassau-Siegen, employed a group of artists, chief among them Albert Eckhout (1610–64) and Frans Post (1612–80). Their watercolours of landscape and plants are both beautiful and accurate. As other gifted Dutch painters followed their lead, the amount of information on the flora and fauna of the East and West Indies grew, and the quality of the studies improved.

Among other talented botanical and landscape artists who used watercolour to record their discoveries were Claude Aubriet (1665–1742), Marie Sibylla Merian (1647–1717), Charles Plumier (1646–1704), a French monk, Sir Hans Sloane (1660–1753), the founder of the British Museum, Mark Catesby (1679–1749) and François Turpin (1775–1840).

Probably Sir Joseph Banks, naturalist and president of the British Royal Society, did most to encourage artists to join exploratory and scientific expeditions. When Captain James Cook set out on his first voyage into the Pacific in 1768, he had with him, at Banks's instigation, two artists: Alexander Buchan for the topographical work and Sidney Parkinson as a natural history painter. The watercolours of Parkinson (1745–71) who, on the death of Buchan, had to take over the topographical studies as well, are among the best of their kind. William Hodges (1744–97) was the artist on Cook's second voyage and John Webber (1752–98) on the third. Webber, a close observer of nature, took back to England so complete a record of the expedition that a later writer wrote, 'no voyage undertaken in the days before photography ever returned so well documented with pictorial illustrations.'

When HMS *Beagle* arrived at Falmouth in 1836 after a five-year scientific voyage she had aboard a comprehensive visual account of the expedition, including a great many lively watercolour drawings, and also of course, Charles Darwin, who had accumulated much of the evidence for his theory of evolution by natural selection, later published in his *The Origins of Species*. The professional artist on the *Beagle* was Augustus Earle who, when his health broke down in 1833, was replaced by Conrad Martens, 'an excellent landscape drawer . . . a pleasant person, and like all birds of that class, full up to the neck with enthusiasm'. Martens was a fine painter; his *The Beagle in Murray Narrow, Beagle Channel* is a lovingly observed example of free watercolour painting.

During the voyage of HMS *Challenger* in 1872–75 the official artist, J. J. Wild, and the gifted amateurs aboard produced numerous drawings and watercolours of the people and places they visited, as well as exhaustive studies of marine life (one of the main purposes of the expedition). Apart from the work of Wild and the naturalists Henry Mosely and John Murray, Lieutenant Pelham Aldrich kept a journal that is full of expressive and sometimes beautiful thumbnail watercolour sketches. Freely treated, they have a liveliness and charm that is missing in the more finished studies of the professionals.

Mt. Lister, Sept. 16, 1911. Evening. A watercolour made by Edward Wilson during the ill-fated expedition of Captain Scott to the South Pole (Scott Polar Research Institute, Cambridge)

29

Following the Sun

There was an old Derry-down-Derry,
Who loved to see little folks merry;
    So he made them a Book
    And with laughter they shook
At the fun of this Derry-down-Derry.

Edward Lear (1812–88), Derry-down-Derry, known and loved by all for his *Book of Nonsense*, was truly a man of many parts; a fine nature illustrator, confident draughtsman, writer and brilliant watercolour artist. His sure eye, confident line and graceful handling of colour were barely appreciated in his time, and even today he is best remembered for his limericks and for the fact that he taught drawing to Queen Victoria.

Many artists have been lured to foreign parts in search of new subject matter, a different light and colours, or merely to escape their creditors, but few have had the wanderlust of Edward Lear. From the age of twenty-five, Lear was a wanderer; never settling long in one place, he roamed the Mediterranean and the Near East; he was an old man when he made a trip to India and Sri Lanka. His travels were motivated by love of natural beauty and excitement at discovering new landscape subjects. Often unwell, he pushed on with dogged determination to reach places that would tax the stamina of the fittest man.

The view was his chief reward. The sense of awe he felt for nature is apparent in his description of a mountain in Italy: 'Wild spires of stone shoot up into the air, barren and clearly defined, in the form of a gigantic hand against the sky, and in the crevices and holes of this fearfully savage pyramid the houses of Pentedatilo are wedged, while darkness and terror brood over all the abyss around this, the strangest of human abodes.'

Born the same year as Charles Dickens, Edward Lear was the twentieth child of Ann and Jeremiah Lear, a stockbroker who was also connected with sugar refining. When he was four his father's business failed and he was entrusted to his sister, Ann, who fortunately had a private income of £300 a year, left to her by her grandmother. Twenty-one years his senior, Ann mothered this delicate

View of Jerusalem. Edward Lear (Tate Gallery, London)

boy; Lear suffered from bronchitis, asthma and, from the age of six, frequent attacks – as many as eighteen a month – of epilepsy, which were a source of worry and distress throughout his life. His own gallant description for his affliction was 'The Morbids'.

Stairs leading to S. Pietro in Vincoli. Edward Lear, 1812-1888 (Tate Gallery, London)

Impressed by Turner's paintings at Petworth House in Sussex, Lear had by the age of sixteen decided to be a landscape artist. Living with his sister in a top-floor flat in London, he supplemented their income by selling the occasional drawing for a few shillings and making, as he put it, 'morbid disease drawings, for hospitals and certain doctors of physic'. By the age of twenty he had produced his *Illustrations of the Family of Psittacidae*, forty-two coloured lithographs of parrots, still considered one of the most sensitive and accurate illustrated works of natural history ever produced, comparable with Audubon. There followed a period living under the patronage of Lord Stanley at Knowsley Hall in Lancashire, making drawings for a work on the unique menagerie on the estate. It was here that Lear discovered a talent for nonsense verse and began his famous book of limericks. In July 1837, his health deteriorating, he set off for Rome and a milder climate. During his three-month trip through Bavaria, followed by equally leisurely visits to Milan and Florence, he caught the wanderlust that was never to leave him. He arrived in Rome with a bulging portfolio of sketches and watercolours, but he was soon off to Sicily. Over the next few years he made copious watercolours of the Ionian Islands, Greece and Albania. Then came visits to Corsica, Turkey, Egypt and the Holy Land, where he made a beautiful watercolour of Petra. Ever modest, he wrote, 'I have found a new world – but my art is helpless to recall it to others, or to represent it to those who have never seen it.'

At the age of sixty-one he began his two-year tour of India and Sri Lanka and although delighted with what he saw ('O fruits! O flowers! O vegetables!'), the enormously long train journeys and abrupt changes of climate took their toll of both his temper and his health. Nevertheless, he made around six hundred drawings as well as filling nine sketch books. A violent attack of lumbago caused him to break off his tour and return to Europe, where he settled in San Remo until his death in 1888.

Although Lear was not the most accomplished of the topographical landscape painters working at the time, in his ability to capture the atmosphere of a scene and put it down boldly and simply he was second only to Turner. His work is spontaneous, sensitive and 'modern', belying his own estimate of himself: 'I cannot but know that there is a vein of poetry within me that ought to have come out – though I begin to doubt that it ever will.'

Walls of Ancient Samos, Cephalonia. Edward Lear. Despite his disabilities, Lear was drawn to near-inaccessible views (Private Collection)

30

Marine Watercolours

Opposite top: *Shipping Becalmed.* J. C. Schetky, 'Old Sepia, 1778-1874 (National Maritime Museum, London)

Opposite bottom: *Calais Pier.* David Cox (Whitworth Art Gallery, University of Manchester)

Below: *Yarmouth Roads.* J. M. W. Turner. The fury of the storm is expressed in a vortex of sky and water (Walker Art Gallery, Liverpool)

'The sea has never been, and I fancy, will never be or can be painted; it is only suggested by means of a more or less spiritual and intelligent conventionalism.' Ruskin's opinion notwithstanding, many watercolour artists have devoted all their efforts to painting seascapes. Indeed, most of the great British watercolourists have, at some time or other, endeavoured to capture the sea in its various moods: the play of light over water in a calm; the buffeting of a Channel packet in a stiff breeze; the cruel frenzy of a storm at sea with spume-crested waves hurling themselves at the sky. Turner of all artists came nearest to defying Ruskin's words. In *Yarmouth Roads*, a steamship batters its way from Yarmouth against a heaving sea; sky and water meet; the fury of the storm is expressed in the vortex of crest and trough.

In Europe, it was the Dutch marine artists of the mid-17th century who first attempted to capture the surge and movement of the sea and its capricious changes of mood, striving to depict on canvas and paper the mass and tensions of water. Before, the sea had been represented as a series of evenly spaced, jagged waves, having little effect on the ships sailing upon its surface. There had been no attempt at movement and atmosphere, no close observation of the formation of waves, no effort to depict the romance of turbulent water.

Ludolf Bakhuyzen (1631–1708), one of the pioneers of marine painting, would go to sea in the roughest weather to study at first

Seascape with Men-of-War. John Cantiloe Joy, 1856 (National Maritime Museum, London)

hand the configuration of storm-tossed waves. The Van de Veldes, father and son, who carried on the tradition, settled in England in 1672 at the invitation of Charles II, and each received a salary of £100 per annum 'for taking and making Draughts of sea fights'.

The realism of the Van de Veldes exerted only a limited influence on contemporary marine painters. Throughout the 18th century most of the paintings of sea battles showed ships correct in every detail of sail, rigging and decoration, but lifeless, wallowing in static seas. Oddly enough it was the discovery of the seaside watering place and the delights of sea bathing in the latter part of the 18th century that drew the attention of artists to the infinite variety of the sea. In the eyes of the public, the sea with its ever-changing moods carried the same romance as snow-capped mountains, stately oaks and quaint ruins. Romantic artists seized upon this subject matter.

One early marine artist who was influenced by the Van de Veldes was Peter Monamy (1670–1749). Born in Jersey, he was apprenticed to a London house painter with premises on London Bridge. The young Channel Islander, fascinated by the constant flow of river traffic on the Thames, began to make watercolour drawings of riverside scenes in the manner of the Dutch artists. His almost monochrome treatment, with its pale blue tints, warm browns and a suggestion of red, was the first sign of the great marine paintings of fifty years later. Other painters of seascapes followed, among them Samuel Scott (1702–72), Charles Brooking (1723–59), Charles Gore (1747–86) and John Clevely (1747–86). But it was the next generation, born toward the end of the 18th century, who really began to imbue their seascapes with movement, atmosphere and a sense of turbulent water. A love of the subject, coupled with keen observation and great dexterity in handling the medium, was combined in these artists to produce vibrant watercolours that have rarely been surpassed.

J. C. Schetky (1778–1874), known as Old Sepia to his pupils at the Royal Naval College, Portsmouth, because of his fondness for working in brown ink, could produce some astonishing effects in monochrome studies. He loved the sea. Affecting the role of a sailor, he always dressed in blue and carried a boatswain's 'call' which he would pipe to weigh anchor when he went on sketching expeditions in his own boat. Famous in his day, he was appointed marine artist in ordinary to Queen Victoria.

Constable, with his entrenched love of the English countryside, once wrote that in his opinion boats were uninteresting and 'so little capable of the beautiful sentiment that belongs to landscapes that they have done a great deal of harm'. This sentiment did not prevent him painting brilliant watercolour seascapes. His studies made at Yarmouth, Harwich, Brighton and Folkstone show a sensitive awareness that belies his words. A tiny watercolour sketch, no more than 5 x 8 in. (12.7 × 20.3 cm), *Shipping on the Orwell*, captures all the atmosphere of a bustling river estuary.

John Sell Cotman often tore himself away from landscape subjects to paint the Norfolk wherries and fishing boats busy on their native waterways, bringing to his pictures the same control of colour, tone and light and shade. Although a number of his marine paintings in watercolour appear overworked to modern eyes, they were in their day more acceptable to the public, who delighted in the accurate portrayal of ships and boats. In *The Needles*, Cotman created one of

Bridlington Harbour. A. V. Copley-Fielding, 1787-1855 (Whitworth Art Gallery, University of Manchester)

his most accomplished pictures. The packetboat from France, anchoring off the Isle of Wight, allowed him the opportunity to note down an idea which he later turned into a watercolour of great simplicity and beauty. Executed with seeming ease, using only a few colours, it conveys a sense of unity and atmosphere missing in many of his more consciously constructed studies.

David Cox's bold and vigorous watercolour technique was well suited to breezy seascapes: scudding clouds above restless, choppy seas. In *Calais Pier*, one of his most dramatic seascapes, dashing waves break against the jetty, covering with spray the passengers huddled together awaiting the arrival of the Dover packet.

In his day, A. V. Copley-Fielding (1787–1855) was considered one of the best if not *the* best marine artist by his contemporaries. Ruskin said of him, 'No man has ever given, with the same flashing freedom, the race of a running tide under a stiff breeze; nor caught, with the same grace and precision, the curvature of the breaking wave, arrested or accelerated by the wind.' Unfortunately he tended to paint to a formula, using the same elements time after time – a fishing smack heeling over in a storm, a buoy, a piece of driftwood and the inevitable seagulls wheeling above. Modern critics are accordingly less complimentary, but his watercolour, *Bridlington Harbour*, in which for once the sea is comparatively calm, is an impressive work which does much to justify Ruskin's eulogy.

Clarkson Stanfield (1793–1867) had the sea in his blood. Nine years spent before the mast gave him his thorough grasp of ships and the way they behave in heavy seas. After leaving the sea through injury, he spent eighteen years as a painter of theatre scenery and dioramas before launching himself as a professional painter of seascapes.

31

Watercolour in America

The growth of watercolour painting in America can be roughly divided into three stages. To begin with the medium was regarded as a poor relation of oil painting, at best useful for studies or private satisfaction. By and large it was thought necessary for an aspiring artist to study in Paris, and watercolour has never assumed an important place in French art. In the early years of the 19th century American watercolours closely followed the English school, with little promise of the vast steps that were to be taken by American watercolourists half a century later. Yet even during this period, artists affected by the transition from Neo-Classicism to Romanticism turned to landscape painting, and topographical portfolios of American scenery were fashionable. Artists like George Catlin, Karl Bodmer, Alfred Jacob Miller and Seth Eastman turned westwards for subject matter, depicting the landscape and people of the expanding frontier.

Here was no leisurely Alpine sketching tour. These artists shared unknown hazards and hardships with the pioneer families, covering thousands of miles of prairie in covered wagons or on horseback, canoeing uncharted rivers, and tramping the mountain trails. Although few were painters of the first rank, they nevertheless documented their journeys faithfully, and rarely did they fail to convey a sense of drama and awe. They were artist explorers, often transmitting records of hitherto unknown territory.

The second stage began about 1870 and extended to about 1890. During this period Winslow Homer, and later Maurice Brazil Prendergast and John Singer Sargent, brought new meaning to watercolour painting. It was this generation of artists who crossed the

Below: *Interior of a Mandan Earth Lodge,* painted *c.*1839 by Karl Bodmer, 1809-1893, one of the explorer-artists

Below right: *Comanche Warrior.* George Catlin

Above: *Trappers Resting on the Trail.* Alfred Jacob Miller, 1810-1874.

dividing line between representational drawing and expressive painting. Discarding the carefully accurate drawing of the contemporary English school, these American artists developed a new approach to watercolour, laying on deep, rich tones at a single stroke of the brush in preference to building up tonal contrasts. They appeal immediately to the senses, capturing the smell of the sea, the feel of buffeting winds, the sound of surf, the humid heat of tropical beaches. Their control of draughtsmanship is instant; seldom laboured, it is the result of structural understanding rather than a careful copying.

From 1890 onwards American watercolourists, building on the experience of those of the middle period, developed the medium in expressive ways. No longer restricted by naturalistic interpretation, they used watercolour to express pure emotion; colour formed rhythmical masses, obviating the meticulous rendering of colour in nature.

One of the earliest artists to depict American landscape in watercolour was in fact a Swiss, Karl Bodmer (1809–93), and it was he who did much to popularize the West as a source of subject matter for his American contemporaries. Born near Zurich, he studied painting in Paris until joining a scientific expedition to North America in 1832. The party followed the Missouri to its source near the Canadian border and during this thirteen-month journey Bodmer made accurate watercolour drawings of the Indian tribes – their customs, way of life and dwellings. Still more important were his landscape views along the river. His keenly observed *Forest Scene with Indian Tree Burial, Near Fort Union* shows all the attributes of an English early Romantic work, diffused with an all-over sunlit glow.

There is a perceptibely American element in Bodmer which became more pronounced in the work of Alfred Jacob Miller (1810–74). Miller, who was born in Baltimore, studied art in Paris, and the

influence of the French Romantic painters is obvious. His Indians ride 'chargers', thoroughbred Arabs with staring eye, flared nostril, gracefully arched neck and streaming mane and tail – a far cry from the rangy ponies of the prairie. Miller, the most obviously romantic of the early American watercolourists, looked for grandeur in his landscapes and saw the Indian as an idealized 'noble savage' in the tradition of Jean Jacques Rousseau. Even the titles of his paintings sound a Romantic note: *A Bourgeois of the Rocky Mountains, Lake, Wind River, Chain of Mountains.* The watercolours he produced during his trek along the Oregon Trail to the west of the Wind River Mountains are comparable with the Alpine scenes of his European contemporaries. They are strongly drawn, the colour squeezed from a limited palette, and though more Romantic than accurate, they express Miller's own concepts of people and nature.

Of all the painters of the West, Seth Eastman (1808–75) stands out as a major figure in the development of the American watercolour movement. Trained at West Point Military Academy – he eventually became a brigadier general – he devoted much of his time to painting Indians and the scenery along the Mississippi and Ohio rivers. Unlike Miller and his other contemporaries, Eastman was not dominated by a constricting line. He drew with the brush, building up his tones from light to dark with clear, brilliant colour. In his ability to capture

Above: *Little Scheveningen.* James McNeill Whistler (Museum of Fine Arts, Boston. Gift of Walter Gay)

sparkling light he anticipated the work of Winslow Homer and other artists of the late 19th century.

Watercolour painting was not the exclusive preserve of the artist explorers of the West. Others were using the medium to depict more prosaic subjects. E. Leutze (1816–68), T. P. Rossiter (1817–71), John F. Kensett (1818–73) and Thomas Hicks (1823–90), among others, were working more or less conventionally in the medium during this period, but it was Winslow Homer (1836–1910) who widened the bounds of watercolour in a truly novel way.

'Mr. Homer goes in, as the phrase is, for perfect realism, and cares not a jot for such fantastic hair-splitting as the distinction between beauty and ugliness.' Written in 1875, this criticism from Henry James missed the point. By that time Homer had already made a major contribution to the development of American art and by the end of

Left: *Ranelagh Gardens.* James McNeill Whistler (Freer Gallery of Art, Smithsonian Institution, Washington D.C.)

191

Woman Sewing. Winslow Homer (In the Collection of the Corcoran Gallery of Art, Washington D.C. Bequest of James Parmelee)

the century he had transformed watercolour into a powerful, direct medium, creating fresh and vital pictures of great beauty.

Winslow Homer, like a number of his fellow artists of the period, started his career as a printmaker and illustrator, apprenticed to a Boston lithographer. Although he was submitting wood engravings to *Harper's Weekly* by 1857, he did not begin to paint seriously until 1862. Working at the time of the French Impressionists, he was influenced to some extent by Degas and Manet; his *Croquet Scene*, painted in 1866, shows a startling resemblance to Monet's *Women in a Garden*. Homer was attracted to watercolour at an early stage and his work in this medium was always well in advance of his oil paintings. In the 1870s he was still 'drawing' in watercolour – illustrating rather than painting – but his *Boys Wading* of 1873 and *The Sick Chicken* of the following year suggested a deeper approach. By the end of the century he was painting such vigorous watercolours as *Nassau, The Shell Heap* and *Tornado – Bahamas*. In these Bahamian studies, although the form is solidly delineated, light and colour have become almost synonymous. His influence is reflected in the work of his contemporaries, as well as the watercolourists who followed him.

Although best known for his oil portraits, John Singer Sargent (1856–1925) himself believed his watercolours held greater artistic expression. In this he was probably right; only in these was he able to

192

apply the colourful palette of the French Impressionists, achieving a highly suggestive personal romanticism through the manipulation of light and colour.

If Sargent was a success in his lifetime, the same could not be said of his contemporary, Maurice Brazil Prendergast (1859–1924). Fifty years ahead of his time, he met with little acceptance until comparatively recently, though he is now accepted as one of America's first modern masters. His figure studies, patchworks of positive colour, are an exercise in happy pattern making. 'The love you liberate in your work is the only love you keep' – his own words sum up his attitude towards painting.

James McNeill Whistler (1834–1903), another American artist who began as a West Point cadet, was one of the outstanding painters of the late 19th century. He too often worked in watercolour. Born in the United States, he studied in Paris, then settled in London, an expatriate from choice, and his work had more influence on European artists than those of his native land. He set himself up as a character; wit, dandy and exhibitionist, and he was either loved or loathed by those who knew him. His sensitive watercolours, like the rest of his work, were strongly influenced by Japanese art. A passage from a

John Biglen (professional oarsman) in a single scull.

Thomas Eakins

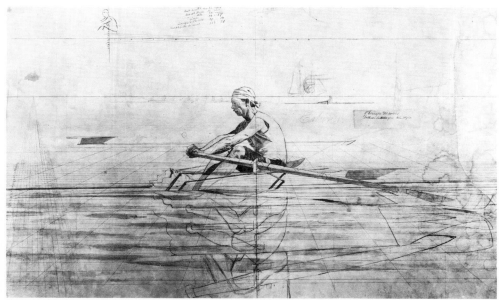

Above: *John Biglen in a Single Scull,* c.1873. Thomas Eakins, 1844-1916 (The Metropolitan Museum of Art, New York. Fletcher Fund, 1924)

Left: Perspective Drawing for *John Biglen in a Single Scull* (Museum of Fine Arts, Boston. Gift of Cornelius V. Whitney)

lecture he gave in 1855 describes his forthright views on art: 'Nature contains the elements, in colour and form, of all pictures, as the keyboard contains the notes of all music. But the artist is to pick and choose, and group with science, these elements, that the result may be beautiful – as a musician gathers his notes, and forms his chords, until he brings forth from chaos glorious harmony. To say to the painter, that Nature is to be taken as she is, is to say to the player, that he may sit on the piano.' Whistler adopted the philosophy of 'art for art's

Opposite: *Venetian Doorway.* John Singer Sargent (The Metropolitan Museum of Art, New York. Gift of Mrs Francis Ormond, 1950)

195

sake'. His watercolours such as *Southend Pier* and *Maude Reading in Bed*, show a remarkable spontaneity, their colour restrained yet clear. In *Ranelagh Gardens*, the combination of clear greens, pale blues and greys, and the masterly control of tone, brilliantly suggest a sunny summer's day – a moment in time captured.

The watercolours of Thomas Eakins (1844–1916) also halt time and motion to capture an instant image, in a similar way to a photograph. His fascination with mechanics and mathematics – when he visited the Paris Exhbition in 1867 he showed more interest in the railway

Maine Island. John Marin, 1870-1953 (The Phillips Collection, Washington, D.C.)

engines and machinery than the art – can most clearly be seen in his series of boating watercolours painted in the early 1870s. For *John Biglen in a Single Scull*, he first prepared a carefully analysed study in pen, pencil and wash, before commencing the actual watercolour. Focal points in the picture are arranged to create a spatial significance, combining verticals, horizontals and diagonals to achieve an almost mathematical composition. Inevitably Eakins's work has none of the movement or spontaneity of Homer's later watercolours, and certainly none of the dash and dynamic vigour of John Marin (1870–1953).

More than any other artist, it was Marin who triggered off the explosion in the growth of American watercolour. His background gives little clue to his eventual development as a pioneer of the adventurous manipulation of the medium. He was brought up in Weehawken, New Jersey, by two maiden aunts. Persuaded to study for a business career he gave it up to become an apprentice to an architect; but this too, was not for him, so his aunts prevailed on his father to allow him to attend a Parisian art school. His early work was conservative, but under the influence of the Futurist movement he

Right: *In Vaudeville: Bicycle Rider*, 1919.
Charles Demuth, 1883-1935 (In the
Collection of the Corcoran Gallery of Art,
Washington, D.C. Bequest of Mr and Mrs
Francis Biddle)

Below left: *Movement, Fifth Avenue*, 1912.
John Marin (The Art Institute of Chicago,
Alfred Stieglitz Collection)

Below right: *Equinoctial*, 1936. Charles H.
Woodbury (In the Collection of the
Corcoran Gallery of Art, Washington,
D.C. Gift of David Woodbury)

steadily developed a swift subjective style. Throwing off
representational imagery, he replaced it with intense perception,
relying on the full use of the senses and giving rein to his natural
romanticism. 'Painting is founded on the heart controlled by the
head', as he put it.

Writing became an extension of Marin's art, which he used in his
own highly individual style to express his copious ideas on his art.
'Art is not so easy – it takes all a man's got – it takes all a man's got
to make it – to have a look of Easiness'. By the 1920s he was regarded
as a great watercolourist in America and by the end of his life his
reputation was worldwide. His influence on the next generation of
American artists was incalculable. Towards the end of his life he
wrote. 'Eighty-three years is a long time. I have had a long life and a

very happy one – retained all my faculties and want to go with them. Why stay?'

During the early part of the 20th century more and more American artists turned to watercolour as a means of expression, working in a multitude of varying styles. Among the best were Arthur Davies, whose romantic landscapes hovered between naturalism and decoration, Childe Hassam, William Hitschel, Gifford Beal, the frankly decorative Rockwell Kent and Sigurd Skou. Subsequent generations of American artists, inspired by the example of Rouault, Dufy, Paul Klee and Egon Schiele, as well as their own native painters, have turned more and more to watercolour, and the contemporary art scene in America abounds with exciting experimental work. Always searching, these artists see in watercolour a mode of expression with greater flexibility than virtually any other medium.

Colour and texture have been exploited to the full by such adventurous colourists as Sam Francis, who achieves a shattering chromatic vibrancy by controlled brushwork, 'spattering', flicks of paint and vertical dribbles allowed to run from top to bottom of the picture. This organized though seemingly chance approach (the great traditional watercolourists were always on the lookout for the 'happy accident') has also been fostered by Jackson Pollock, Mark Tobey and Morris Graves. Figures and watercolour portraits have been variously

Off Stonington, 1921. John Marin (Columbus Museum of Art, Ohio. Gift of Ferdinand Howald)

Above: *Waterfront,* 1942 Lyonel Feininger
(The Phillips Collection, Washington, D.C.)

Right: *Burlesque Theatre, Times Square,* 1940.
Edward Hopper (In the Collection of the
Corcoran Gallery of Art, Washington, D.C.
Museum Purchase, Membership Association
Fund)

200

treated by Andrew Wyeth, Rico Lebrun, Richard Lindner, Larry Rivers and Robert Rauschenberg.

A number of European artists who settled in the United States have had considerable influence on the development of American watercolour. Prominent among them is Ben Shahn, whose paintings of contemporary American life have a luminosity of colour which has affected many of his fellow artists. George Grosz, Hans Hofmann, Willem de Kooning, Yasuo Kuniyoshi and a host of others, have helped to mould the American watercolour tradition. Among home-grown artists who have exerted a marked influence are Max Webber, Robert Motherwell, Lyonel Feininger and Alexander Calder. Among contemporary watercolourists breaking new ground are Jack King, Glen E. Bradshaw, Edward Reep, Leonard Edmondson, Hilda Levy and many, many others.

Above *Lobsterman's Ledge,* 1939. Andrew Wyeth (National Gallery of Art, Washington, D.C. Ailsa Mellon Bruce Fund)

Below: *Hawk Mountain.* Andrew Wyeth (National Gallery of Art, Washington, D.C. Gift of Halleck Lefferts)

Overleaf: *Lute and Molecules.* Ben Shahn (Tate Gallery, London)

32

War in Watercolour

Pictures of war are almost as old as war itself. From ancient times artists have been encouraged, or ordered, to record battles in pictures – usually victories, since few rulers or generals wish to be reminded of their defeats. Egyptian wall frescoes commemorating military victories show the victorious pharaoh and his armies sweeping away hosts of pygmy adversaries. There is certainly no feeling for the horrors of war: the artist was expected to record a scene; it was inconceivable that his personal feelings should intrude.

Column on the March. Christopher Nevinson achieves an intensity of feeling that is noticeably missing from Second World War painting (Imperial War Museum, London)

Headquarter's Room, 1944. Barnett Freedman
(Imperial War Museum, London)

Battles had to be glorious, chivalrous and above all heroic. Renaissance painters flung their soldiers into battle mounted on carefully arranged, plunging horses, with wildly criss-crossing waves of lances. There is more sense of action in Titian's *Battle of Cadore* and Leonardo da Vinci's drawing of the *Battle of Anghiari*, but battle paintings were still splendid, romantic adventures – celebrations of valour – in the 19th century. The Baron Gros glorified Napoleon's victories; Lady Butler immortalized the Thin Red Line and the charge of the Scots Greys at Waterloo – these and a thousand similar paintings were records or testimonies of an action, seen from a distance, with little personal involvement on the part of the artist.

The advent of photography, coupled with the growing emancipation of the literary and visual arts, encouraged a more realistic portrayal of war, with its attendant bloodshed and horror. Photography was first used widely to freeze the images of war during the Crimean War. There was no way of reproducing them except engraving, and it was left to the war artist to send back his sketches and drawings by fast packet, to be engraved on wood overnight ready to appear the following day in the *Illustrated London News*. In this way the public were kept abreast of the progress of a war being fought on the eastern borders of Europe.

A more personal record of the Crimean War was kept by Sir Henry Clifford V.C. a keen and talented amateur watercolourist. At the start of the war he, like the professional war artists depicted the heroic, the intimate and the mildly amusing (his watercolour of *The Light Division Camp at Varna* has the air of a picnic), but as the war dragged on through the fierce Crimean winter, and disease and privation began to take its toll, drawings were going back to England showing the dreadful conditions in the hospitals, the sufferings of underclothed and half-starved troops and the incompetence and often arrogance of the General Staff. War artists had begun to associate themselves with the war.

Clifford painted a number of poignant sketches quite unlike his

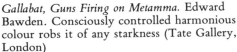

Gallabat, Guns Firing on Metamma. Edward Bawden. Consciously controlled harmonious colour robs it of any starkness (Tate Gallery, London)

earlier heroic studies. His sketch of hundreds of dead and bloated
horses, piled into a shallow valley after the Battle of Inkerman, being
torn by vultures and buzzards, conveys pity and horror. The sense of
pity is equally evident in his *Guarding the Advance Trench during the
Winter of 1854–55*, in which shivering troops wearing 'Balaklava'
helmets huddle together against the driving snow. Another
watercolour shows wood for huts, food and warm clothing being
taken up to the front through the snow on packhorses, with a dead
horse and a half-buried kettle drum beside the path. The hardships of
war, now beginning to be clearly presented to the public, prompted a
satirical cartoon in *Punch*, captioned: '*Well, Jack! Here's good news
from home. We're to have a medal.*' '*That's very kind. Maybe one of
these days we'll have a coat to stick it on.*'

When the Civil War broke out in America in 1861, the tactics used
were those of the Napoleonic campaigns; by the time it finished in
1865, these tactics had changed dramatically, foreshadowing the
methods of the First World War. Photography had made some
progess since Roger Fenton's Crimean shots, and photographers were
able to record incidents in battles and their aftermath more easily.
Many of these reflect the photographers' personal feelings toward the
horror and futility of war; this is clearly apparent in some of the work
in Gardner's *Photographic Sketchbook of the War*. But as yet there
was still no method of photomechanical reproduction, no way of
transferring these photographs into process plates to be printed in
newspapers and periodicals. The public of America and Europe chiefly
relied on the watercolours, drawings and pen-and-wash sketches of the
professional war artists, which were engraved on wooden blocks.
Railways helped but drawings from the South destined for European
newspapers had to run the gauntlet of Union blockade ships. The host
of watercolours, drawings and pen-and-wash sketches produced
during the war varied in quality from that of the enthusiastic amateur
to the work of such artists as Winslow Homer, W. L. Sheppard,
Edward Forbes and Alfred R. Waud.

Two outstanding war artists who covered the Civil War were
Frank Vizetelly and Louis Kurz. Vizetelly, born in London in 1830,

Shelterers in the Tube, 1941. Henry Moore was one of the few war artists of the Second World War to capture fear and foreboding (Tate Gallery, London)

had already had considerable experience as a war artist during the Franco-Austrian War of 1859 when he was commissioned by the *Illustrated London News* to record the American Civil War in pictures. He sent back a number of sketches of the activities of the Union Army, until his wash drawings of the rout at the First Battle of Bull Run put him out of favour with the authorities and the Federal War Department withdrew his permit. Undeterred, Vizetelly followed a secret, 'underground' route through Federal lines and presented himself at Confederate Headquarters at Richmond, where he was welcomed with open arms. Given every facility to get close to the firing line – sometimes too close for comfort – he was, as the only war artist operating in the South, able to make a unique pictorial record of the war from the Confederate point of view. Apart from one exciting trip to England aboard a blockade runner and a hair-raising return, he recorded the Southern cause right up to the end.

Louis Kurz, described in his *New York Times* obituary as 'a widely-known artist and friend of President Lincoln', was born at Salzburg but settled in the United States in 1848. At the outbreak of war he joined the 1st Winsconsin Sharpshooters and was later sent by the President to various camps and battles to make on-the-spot sketches and watercolours that were finally printed as lithographs in up to ten colours. Never as historically accurate as Vizetelly's, Kurz's watercolours are nevertheless fine battle scenes. Though essentially romantic (his wounded fall with Thespian grace and die with heroic style), in his *The Fort Pillow Massacre* he comes close to capturing the barbarism of war and to expressing that anti-war feeling so characteristic of the paintings of the First World War.

The grim reality of world war shattered the brittle beliefs of Marinetti and the Futurists in the glory of war. Such disciples as Christopher Nevinson and Wyndham Lewis, faced with the horror of mutilated men in makeshift dressing stations bandaged with newspapers and dying like flies, produced anti-war paintings of great quality.

Although the First World War was fully recorded in still photograph and film, it is the paintings, particularly the watercolours, that best convey the true atmosphere of the conflict. Those lines of dispirited soldiers, tramping stolidly through acres of mud, past shattered stumps of trees, against livid skies, supplied the subject matter for what we now recognize as great works of art. Some of the finest watercolours were produced by Paul Nash, Henry Lamb, William Orpen (an official Canadian war artist) and Eric Kennington. One curious footnote: camouflage, scientifically designed by academic painters, took on all the appearance of early Cubist art.

Paradoxically, the artists of the Second World War, although they produced watercolours of outstanding quality and beauty, showed none of the intensity of feeling of their First World War counterparts (though some painted both wars). The Second World War, exhaustively recorded for posterity on film, allowed the war artists, both official and freelance, to select and interpret the scenes that attracted them, and the results are more often lyrical than disturbing. (However, Henry Moore's often featureless drawings of fearful, haunted sleepers in the London Underground bring home the grimness of civilian involvement.)

Paul Nash's watercolour, *Bomber in the Corn*, has all the romantic tranquility of a Samuel Palmer, its colour harmonious and pleasing. The wrecked bomber, its broken bits carefully scattered, seems almost incidental to an English landscape painting. Even less warlike is his *Battle of Britain*. Although a magnificent painting in itself, it shows none of the excitement and numbing fear of an aerial dog-fight. Contrails weave an intricate pattern against a serene blue sky in which a phalanx of German bombers is thoughtfully placed to balance the composition. A faint echo of the First World War artists appears in Edward Bawden's *Gallabat: Guns Firing at Metemma*, but the consciously controlled, harmonious colour robs it of any real starkness, and his *Omdurman: Sudan Defence Force* is a frankly academic composition of subtle greys, pinks and orange, with a few stylized figures to give it content; on the horizon, an unlikely figure rides an even more unlikely camel.

The disturbing style of Graham Sutherland creates a real feeling of bomb devastation, missing from John Piper's *Council Chamber, House of Commons 1941* and *Somerset Place, Bath*, which have the attributes of stage sets. Barnett Freedman's *15" Gun Turret, HMS Repulse*, accurate, pleasantly coloured and highly detailed as it is, evokes nothing of the sweating, claustrophobic fear of a gun crew closed up for action. Anthony Gross and Eric Ravilious show more concern in exercising a pleasing watercolour technique than in capturing the harsh realities of war.

Bomber in the Corn. Paul Nash. A romantic English landscape in which the bomber is quite incidental (Tate Gallery, London)

33

Flowers

There is no better medium than watercolour for depicting the texture and nature of flowers – the translucency and brilliance of their petals, their dewy freshness. John Ruskin always maintained that no artist could paint the sea, and it could be said that no one can capture the fragile immediacy of a flower. But in the hands of a master, transparent watercolour, washed across the reflective surface of white paper, comes closest to bringing this about. Chinese and Japanese floral painters were aware of this from early times and strove to attain the essence and spirit of petal and leaf, often achieving it with a single, precise sweep of the brush.

In the West, floral art has generally been naturalistic, the artist paying fine attention to detail of structure. It calls for a degree of contemplation and study on the part of the viewer to become aware of the depth of inquiry and analysis undertaken by the artist – time to acknowledge his skill and appreciate the beauty of his work. Usually there is little immediate visual impact.

When the science of botany is allied to flower painting, as it often

Hibiscus, 1796. Tani Bunchō. This study typifies the simplicity, yet perfect control of the Japanese masters (British Museum, London)

has been since the 11th century, there is an even greater demand for minute accuracy. There are of course numerous exceptions; many European artists have painted flowers and plants for quite different reasons. The flowers in Turner's *Vase of Lilies and Other Flowers* are purely a vehicle for colour and 'flittering' light. The French Symbolist Odilon Redon (1840–1916) and the sumptuous colourist Matthew Smith (1879–1959) revelled in their sensuality and voluptuousness.

In western and central Asia the approach to flower painting has been more decorative, highly stylized floral motifs being a common feature of Islamic art, but some Indian artists painted flowers in a naturalistic manner under later European influence.

Flower painting in the Far East, China and Japan, took an entirely different turn. There it became a serious art form, an aesthetic exercise aimed at capturing the spirit, the very essence of plant and flower. A 'oneness' with nature, brought about by the unity of mind and hand, resulted in a sense of the flower being alive. To the Oriental artist this was true realism. A rigid apprenticeship in brush control, coupled with a philosophical sympathy toward the world of nature, enabled him to convey an accurate impression of life, growth and movement.

Floral art reached a peak in China during the Sung Dynasty (960–1279). Two main styles of colour flower painting had been established in the Five Dynasties Period (907–960) which followed the break up of the T'ang empire. Huang Chüan, working at the court of Shu, adopted an ink outline technique, which he combined with the use of bright, positive colour. In the south, Hsü Hsi painted in more restrained washes of ink and colour.

The Emperor Hui Tsung (1101–26), himself a painter as well as a discerning patron with a love of flower and bird paintings, encouraged his court artists to follow the style of Huang Chüan. Throughout Chinese floral art, it has usually been the custom to show flowers accompanied by birds or insects; rarely are they shown by themselves as in European botanical studies. The Emperor strongly believed that the secret of perfection lay in observation, and he was in the habit of awarding prizes to those of his artists who most faithfully painted what they saw. But however lifelike the drawing of a flower appears, it still remains a two-dimensional representation of a living three-dimensional form, and it is only by subtle and cunning techniques that the artist can convince the viewer. Such was the intensity of vision of the Sung painters, that their convention of outlining in black ink goes almost unnoticed, lost in the artist's own conviction. Later Chinese floral works, although showing great beauty and skill, lacked the intense awareness and union with nature evident in the work of the Sung painters. Still later, as European influences filtered into China, there were numerous examples of plants and flowers painted in a Western 'botanical' manner.

The plant and flower works of Japanese scholar painters at first followed closely those of their Chinese counterparts, but gradually a national style evolved, one that was consciously tasteful, softer and less sharp in outline. The decorative style that appeared in the 16th century is probably seen at its best in Japanese paper screens, particularly those of Nakamura Hōchū of the Rimpa school. Painting directly on to a gold or silver paper background, his flowers glow with sunlight and appear natural and totally authentic, despite the artificiality of their gold or silver setting. An impressive Japanese flower painting which shows the simplicity yet perfect control of the masters is *Hibiscus*, painted by Tani Bunchō in 1796. Using only ink and pink pigment, he miraculously conveys a sense of a wide colour range. The beautiful soft brushwork, with its infinitely subtle gradations, creates this impression in the eye of the beholder.

Border of Floral Motifs – from the *Hastings Hours* by the School of the Master of Mary of Burgundy (British Library, London)

211

The common Provence Rose.

Above: *Young Woman and a Lotus Bloom.*
Mughal painting (British Museum, London)

Above right: *The Common Provence Rose.* G.
D. Ehret (Victoria and Albert Museum,
London)

The ability of Chinese and Japanese artists to suggest colour is best expressed in monochrome ink painting. The art of ink painting, in Japanese *Sumi e* (black picture), depends for its effect entirely on subtle nuances of tone, wash gradations, and calligraphic precision of brushwork. Bamboo lends itself as an ideal subject for ink painting, and schools of bamboo painting arose in both China and Japan. It is interesting to compare the subtle difference in treatment between the countries; both are drawn with a single, perfectly controlled brush stroke, but that of the Japanese school is softer, less precise than that of the Chinese.

Though the use of plants and flowers as decorative motifs dates back to ancient times, it was not until the introduction of herbals, in which they were discussed for their medicinal properties and needed to be identified, that they were drawn sufficiently accurately to be recognized. Since then flowering plants have been an important subject of Western art. The *Carrara Herbal*, prepared for Francesco Carrara, Lord of Padua in the late 14th century, and painted by an unknown artist, is one of the earliest works in which plants are portrayed with convincing naturalism. These sensitive and accurate watercolours represent a complete breakaway from the traditional, stylized treatment of the Middle Ages. By the beginning of the 15th century Dürer's intense concern with observation and knowledge was producing plant drawings of arresting beauty, such as his *Great Turf* and *Iris*, both indisputable masterpieces. Jacques Le Moyne made a set of elegant watercolours of flowers and fruit then common in English gardens; he also used naturalistic flower studies in his more fanciful allegorical and pseudo-historical paintings, like *Daughter of the Picts*.

Travellers in unexplored lands often made impressive watercolours of the new plants, flowers and fruits they encountered. Some of these have been mentioned in Chapter 28. By the 18th century enthusiastic botanists were making their own trips to such treasure troves of wild flowers as South Africa and South America, returning with beautiful studies as well as actual specimens.

One of the most important figures in flower painting was the watercolourist and engraver Pierre-Joseph Redouté, who was active at the end of the 18th century. He produced flower paintings and stipple engravings, hand-coloured with transparent watercolour, that rank among the most technically accomplished as well as the most beautiful ever made.

The tradition of floral art has persisted right up to the present day, some artists treating the subject in a traditional, naturalistic manner, others as a base for more adventurous work, exploring colour, texture and abstract pattern.

Canterbury Bell. Pierre Joseph Redouté, one of the greatest European flower painters active at the end of the eighteenth century (Victoria and Albert Museum, London)

213

34

Watercolour in the Theatre

Theatre has always been a rich source of subject matter for watercolour, in addition to being the favourite medium of theatrical designers over the centuries, both for costume and scenery. Other artists, prominent among them Toulouse-Lautrec, Degas and Walter Sickert, were enchanted by theatre, music hall and cabaret and created studies which in themselves were pictures of great beauty. From early times, theatrical entertainment, whether singing, dancing or mummer's play, has offered a fascinating world of make believe which has been echoed in flamboyant, often improbable designs and costumes – until stark realism caught up with the theatre in the 20th century.

The first watercolours of theatrical entertainment are to be found in Egyptian papyrus. Although artistically attractive, they have little of the sophistication of Greco-Roman theatre, but apart from decoration on vases, there is very little visual record of the Greek tragedies, 'satyr' plays and comedies. Surviving frescoes show that these types of plays were popular in Rome, and one example at Boscoreale, painted about 40 BC, shows the stage scenery traditionally used for each of the three types of play. It is intricate and detailed, though the perspective is somewhat wayward here and there, and elegantly coloured, suggesting how Roman painters attracted and entertained their audience.

Illustrations of animal dancers and mummers appear in many early

Watercolour study for the set of *Schéhérazade.* Leon Bakst, one of the leading designers for Diaghilev (Theatre Museum, Victoria and Albert Museum, London)

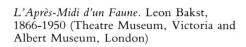
medieval manuscripts, but these mystery plays were performed in front of churches without scenery. By the middle of the 16th century scenery and costume were becoming more and more elaborate. In 1547 Hubert Cailleau produced twenty-six magnificent watercolours for a manuscript of a play based on Arnoul de Grebau's *Mystère de la Passion*, produced at Valenciennes. The colour is restrained except for the devils leaving the entrance to Hell. The stage setting for Hell reads, 'Opening its gullet it let out fire and smoke with devils of horrible shape, and Lucifer rising up high on a dragon shooting fire and smoke from its mouth', and in Cailleau's illustration rich reds combine with blues and greens to astonish and horrify the audience.

Gradually over the centuries costume and scenery became more complex and more elegant, and by the middle of the 17th century drawings from the Turin Ballet had high artistic merit. An intricate watercolour of the Teatro Ducale in Turin, painted in 1681, has all the qualities of a romantic English watercolour of the late 18th century in its brushwork and application of colour without a constricting line.

Art in, and of, the theatre continued to develop along purely realistic lines, and it was not until the very end of the 19th century that design and expression found an entirely new form. It was during this era that the most colourful and exciting designs were produced, and the impetus of the new movement came from Russia.

The demand for a new expression stemmed from an art review, *Mir Iskusstva*, 'The World of Art', a journal edited by Sergei

Watercolour, scenery for *The Nutcracker*.
Alexandre Benois, 1870-1960

Diaghilev, which first appeared in 1899. Diaghilev was the guiding
spirit, but the membership of the 'World of Art' movement included
many established and talented painters who later turned to design for
the theatre. They included Konstantin Somov (1869–1939), Ivan
Bilibine (1870–1950) and Dimitri Filosov (1872–1942), but by far the
most important were Alexandre Benois (1870–1960) and Leon Bakst
(1866–1924). These two artists turned opera and ballet into rich,
colourful spectacle, and the intense, often startling colour they used
did much to free the theatre from mundane realism. Under the
direction of Diaghilev, who introduced the Imperial Russian Ballet to
Paris in 1909, Russian painters changed the whole attitude to ballet
design and made a resounding impact on Western audiences.

Leon Bakst, a one-time fashion designer, was a master of symbolic
colour, which he could contrive to express dramatic meaning, adding a
poetic suggestiveness to music and dance. The colour in each of the
ballets he designed fitted perfectly with subject and choreography,
creating an exotic experience that stunned Western European
theatregoers. His paintings and designs for *Schéhérazade*, music by
Rimsky-Korsakov, are almost unbelievably rich; never before had such
colour been used in the theatre.

Bakst's intensive study of Persian art was translated into his own
idiom: a voluptuous range of reds and orange rubbed shoulders with
blues against black, greens against pinks, pale mauves against gold.
Totally sensuous, it complemented the exotic music and movement.
On the other hand, in his design for the costume of the Faun for
Nijinsky's erotic ballet, *L'Après-Midi d'un Faune* (1912), he used
subdued, tertiary colour to evoke Debussy's music. Even in his
watercolours for a prosaic interior, Bakst lifted the scene from the
ordinary by a use of voluptuously coloured furnishings: curtains of

216

cerulean blue, ultramarine and black; a vermilion bird cage and a sofa splendidly upholstered in red, elephant grey and yellow ochre.

Alexandre Benois wrote the book and designed both costumes and sets for Diaghilev's *Petrushka*, music by Stravinsky. In this ballet all the elements, music, design and choreography (by Fokine), were perfectly balanced to create one of the great masterpieces of ballet. Combining realism and symbolism, with harmonious colour contrasts, Benois brilliantly captured the atmosphere of the tragicomic story of the love of a puppet, Petrushka, for a painted doll, who is infatuated with the Moor, resplendent in gold, pomegranate pink, orange and acid green. Benois's pre-Lenten fair in Admiralty Square, St Petersburg, is filled with whirling, colourful figures, and is real and believable despite, or because of, his nonfigurative colour.

Fired by the imagination of the designers of Diaghilev's Ballet Russe, Picasso, Matisse, Braque, Derain, Juan Gris, Salvador Dali, Clavé, Marie Laurencin, Miro, Rouault, Max Ernst and Léger, all turned to theatrical set design. Marc Chagall's painting for the frontcloth of Stravinsky's *Firebird* was an inspired interpretation of the half-human, half-avian central character, but all these artists worked for the theatre as a sideline, never with the total commitment of Bakst and Benois. Among the designers who came later, Leslie Hurry stands out for his surrealistic interpretations; his watercolour for *Hamlet* displays all the force and dynamism of a William Blake. Among contemporaries, David Hockney is just one who has made fruitful forays into theatrical design.

Watercolour, scenery for *Petrushka,* for Diaghilev's Ballet Russe. Benois (Theatre Museum, Victoria and Albert Museum, London)

35

Delacroix and French Romanticism

'Art should aim at noble simplicity and calm grandeur,' said Winckelmann (*Reflections on the Imitation of Greek Art*, written in 1755), summing up the Classical approach to painting. The Romantic movement was, among other things, a revolt against this belief. To appeal to the head or the heart? To offer a calm contemplation of beauty, or arouse and excite emotions? This has been the dilemma of artists throughout history and often, as in the case of such masters as Raphael, Classicism and Romanticism coexist. During the mid-18th century, this division became more clearly defined. The Romantic rebellion against Greco-Roman Classicism as filtered through the Renaissance spread throughout the arts, and nowhere was it more powerful than in France. The rising importance of landscape painting, which before the beginning of the 19th century had been regarded as a minor art form, did much to bring about these changes in attitude. Through a close study of nature and an effort to depict atmosphere and light, artists drew away from descriptive painting and sought to convey visual experiences that later culminated in abstract art.

In France the Romantic movement, at first mainly literary, was both ferocious and committed. In an attempt to excite the emotions, artists painted scenes of bloodshed and violence, heightening the effect

Guard Room Interior, 1836. Eugène Delacroix, 1798-1863 (Oskar Reinhart Collection, Winterthur)

by aggressive use of colour, exaggerated movement and heavy emphasis on light and shade. Théodore Géricault (1791–1824), one of the leaders of the movement, in whom emotional restlessness, a preoccupation with death and an adulation of natural forces – all characteristics of the Romantic movement – are strongly apparent, was greatly influenced by Jean-Antoine Gros, known as the Baron Gros, a curious and tragic figure.

As the official painter to Napoleon Bonaparte, Gros was given the military title of Inspecteur aux Revues, with a uniform to go with it, which years later he donned to commit suicide. His narratives of the Emperor's victories were a mixture of propaganda, romantic pomp and horror. This is particularly noticeable in *Napoleon on the Battlefield of Eylau*, in which Bonaparte looks modestly heavenwards, magnificently uniformed marshals sit plunging chargers and stiffened corpses litter a snowy foreground.

It was from Gros that Géricault acquired his predilection for prancing horses. Although he rarely, if ever, painted in watercolour for its own sake, his studies, made over ten months, for his masterpiece, *The Raft of the Medusa*, are both moving and disturbing. But Géricault died young and his friend Delacroix, who is said to have posed for one of the central figures on the raft, had far more influence on French watercolour.

Eugène Delacroix (1798–1863) was the greatest of the Romantic painters, though he would not have cared for that label. He was himself surrounded in romance from the very beginning. As his father had been medically certified as being incapable of having children in 1797, the true paternity of the boy, born the following year, has always been a matter of conjecture. It is possible that the subtle and devious statesman Talleyrand was the true father; there was certainly a

The Horse, Isabella and a White Horse. Eugène Delacroix (Private Collection)

Leaving the Stable. Théodore Géricault, 1791-1824 (Museé des Beaux – Arts, Rouen)

marked physical likeness between the two men. By the time Delacroix entered the studio of Guérin in 1815, both his mother and father had died, leaving him and his elder sister impoverished.

Despite his radical approach to painting, Delacroix was at heart conservative, quite willing to accept the patronage of such 'Establishment' figures as Talleyrand and Thiers, who were instrumental in obtaining commissions from the state for the young painter. After the 1848 Revolution, he wrote to George Sands, 'The liberty won at so high a price is not true liberty. True liberty consists of being able to think, of being able to dine at the proper times, and of many other advantages for which political agitation has no respect. Please forgive these reactionary thoughts of mine. . . .' Yet this was the artist who painted *Liberty Leading the People* (over a pile of corpses!). Many of his best-known works in oils involve death or bloodshed, but this is far from common in his watercolours.

Delacroix's friend Soulier, who had been educated in England, introduced him to watercolour painting, which he soon came to regard as a highly expressive medium. Later, the works of Turner – a friend of Delacroix while in Paris – and Bonington gave impetus to the art of watercolour in France (Chateaubriand had already made landscape painting fashionable after his visit to Norwich in 1795).

In 1825, Delacroix visited England for the first time, and in 1852 made a second visit to perfect his watercolour technique. He met Bonington whose paintings of Moorish women stirred his imagination and encouraged him to make the visit to Morocco that was to mark the turning point in his career. While in England he made numerous studies of horses, chief among them *White Stallion Frightened by Lightning*, a watercolour full of power and dynamic movement. Half-crazed with fear, the horse rears, slashing at the air with its hooves, its mane and tail streaming in the wind. Delacroix, who had already reworked the background of one of his pictures after seeing Constable's *The Haywain* when it was exhibited at the 1824 Paris Salon, became even more interested in the Englishman's use of broken colour when he visited him in 1825. Between them, Bonington and Constable had a considerable influence on Delacroix, which is most noticeable in his watercolour landscapes. In these there is none of the violent movement and ferocity of so many of his oils. They have a freshness of colour and a spontaneous sureness of touch. *Landscape near London* is a typical example of the immediate, closely observed landscape vignettes he made in England.

In 1832, Delacroix visited Morocco, where he was captivated by the colour and scintillating light. Like Turner in Venice, he filled sketchbook after sketchbook with hectic notes and keen watercolour studies, many of which he later turned into major works. These pages, crammed with written and visual information, are themselves works of art. Delacroix brought a simplicity to his watercolours, a directness, that seems startlingly modern. In his *Landscape near Tangier* the washes are applied quickly and precisely; the foreground plants are drawn with the brush and the rapidly sketched pencil guidelines are often ignored. The colours are muted yet clear, the tones carefully and subtly controlled, but the buildings, left as white silhouettes, give the study an eye-catching accent. *Landscape in the Pyrenees* is more vigorous, both in colour and treatment; the tones are more pronounced and give it a sombre, brooding quality; the sky is clearly influenced by Constable. At the time he was convalescing in the mountains from an attack of tubercular laryngitis, a disease from which he eventually died.

Artillery Officer. Théodore Géricault (Bührle Collection, Winterthur)

36

Impressionist Watercolours

'Don't proceed according to rules and principles, but paint what you observe. . . Paint generously and unhesitatingly, for it is best not to lose the first impression' (Camille Pissarro).

When Louis Leroy, art critic of *Le Charivari*, coined the term 'impressionist', he was using it to express derision for a painting by Claude Monet, *Impression: Sunrise*, exhibited at the first Impressionist exhibition of 1874. The name stuck and nowadays we accept it naturally to describe that school of young artists who broke away from French Salon painting in the 1870s. But long before, the word 'impression' had appeared frequently in the writings of Corot,

Marine. Édouard Manet, 1832-1883
(Hahnloser Collection)

Constable and members of the Barbizon school, many of whom had already sought to record an instant in time through accurate observation. Constable, who believed that painting could be approached scientifically, made many painstaking studies of skies, writing in the exact time of day and the direction of the wind. To him, as to Pissarro, an impression meant the faithful rendering of a scene passing before his eyes – as he saw it, not as he knew it to be. (Many Romantics, among them Turner, would have argued that an 'impression' was an image retained in the mind after quitting a scene.)

Today we view Impressionist paintings with an easy, instant enjoyment that makes it all the more difficult to conceive the controversy that raged between these artists and their critics for thirty years. Yet this was no deliberately conceived movement. The Impressionists laid down no principles; they produced no manifestos as that combative realist Courbet did. They were simply a group of artists, friends with widely dissimilar backgrounds, experiences and temperaments, who were drawn together by a similar attitude towards the nature of painting. Profoundly affected by Courbet's beliefs, they rejected conventions in painting which they believed had become meaningless and repetitive. To them, traditional art was based on the misconception that form was created by a slow transition from light to shade, created, moreover, under artificial conditions in an artist's studio. Objects seen *en plein air*, in the harsh contrasts of sunlight, had no such roundness or solidity; their contours were blurred by shadow and distance; the shadows were full of colour, never uniformly grey.

They also noticed that objects seen in the open ceased to have their own individual colour, but became a series of tonal masses blended together optically. From this they drew the conclusion that colour as an independent quality did not exist, but was merely the effect of the play of light upon form. Shadow, which in the past had been regarded as a negation of light, was in fact an altered form of it, made up of surrounding primary colours to form a complementary tone. This led the Impressionists to restrict themselves to a palette of spectrum colours only. They set out to paint light, depicting it according to atmosphere and reflection, modifying it in relationship to the colour of the surroundings. Even in their oil paintings they used what was essentially a watercolour technique, allowing the ground to come through, acting as a reflective surface to lend the painting luminosity.

Many of the Impressionists' ideas had been explored by earlier painters, and they acknowledged that they owed a debt to Constable, Corot, Courbet, Boudin, Jongkind and particularly Delacroix. In his later work, Delacroix's approach to colour was influenced by the theories of a French chemist, Eugène Chevreul, who maintained that colours in close proximity modify each other and could be mixed optically. The Impressionists took Delacroix's use of colour a stage further; by placing dabs of colour next to each other, they not only suggested form, but created atmospheric vibration. Constable had already worked along these lines, as Delacroix recorded in his journal. 'Constable says that the superiority of the greens in his meadows is due to the fact that they are made up of a large number of different greens (in close proximity not mixed). What gives a lack of intensity and life to the ordinary run of landscape painters is that they do it with a uniform tint.'

Watercolour, never a popular medium in France, had been introduced into the country earlier in the century by French artists working in England who had rubbed shoulders with Girtin, Constable and Turner. Delacroix, who discovered that watercolour could be a highly expressive medium, was encouraged by a young Englishman in

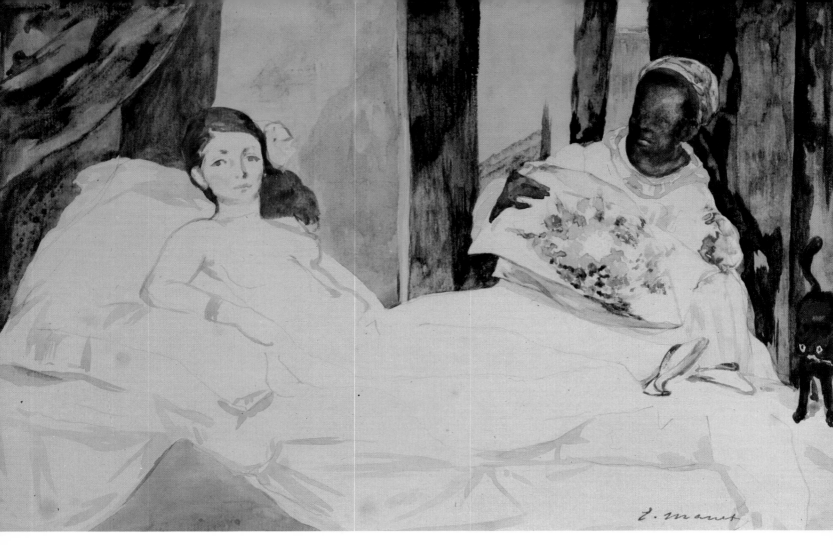

Olympia. Édouard Manet. A watercolour study for the final painting (Niarchos Collection)

France, Richard Parkes Bonington (1802–28). Through Delacroix, Bonington had a marked influence on the Impressionists, who found watercolour an ideal medium for capturing the instant image.

Bonington's father, on losing his post as governor of Nottingham gaol in 1797, set himself up as a drawing master in the town, and when he married in 1801 his wife opened a school for young ladies. Together they made a prosperous living until the introduction of the factory system into the lace-making industry caused a dramatic slump in the number of pupils and they were forced to close the school. In 1817 the family, along with numerous other Nottingham people, slipped across to France, taking with them the forbidden lace machines. There, Bonington senior opened up a lace factory with himself as designer. His son Richard was meant to become a designer of lace in the family business, but the fifteen-year-old boy had other ideas. He spent all his spare time sketching in the streets and on the quays of Calais, and it was there that a French watercolourist, Louis Francia, recognized his talent and took him under his wing. Francia had worked with Girtin in England and found Bonington an apt pupil, quick to learn and possessing an instinctive grasp of colour. Despite parental opposition, Bonington, encouraged by Francia, went to study art in Paris at the studio of Baron Gros. Francia also gave him an introduction to Delacroix. It is difficult to determine the influence each had upon the other, but later Delacroix remarked of Bonington's painting that 'nobody in the modern school, and probably no one before him, possessed the lightness of execution, which particularly in watercolour makes his work, as it were, diamond-like; charming and seducing the eye, independently of the actual subject or imitation.'

Watercolour was still considered an English novelty. Bonington used it to explore the infinite possibilities of the play of light and shadow on landscape and buildings. His fresh, sparkling open-air effects, his brilliance of colour, his glittering seascapes, came as startling innovations to contemporary French painters accustomed to building up their pictures in terms of tone rather than colour. Even Baron Gros, who generally insisted that 'drawing comes first, colour second', referred to Bonington's watercolours as 'streaming with light'. Corot said that the sight of a Bonington watercolour in a shop window determined his choice of career. From about 1824, to his tragically premature death from consumption four years later, Bonington used the tip of his brush to hatch colour with quick, bold strokes. This, together with his technique of dragging a dry brush across the rough surface of the paper, became the hallmark of his later work. Among the following generation, Eugène Boudin (1824–98), Johan-Berthold Jongkind (1819–91), Jean-Baptiste Camille Corot (1796–1875) and Gustave Courbet (1819–77) continued the practice of sketching in watercolour out of doors and experimenting with light and colour. Although they were conscious of the overall importance of light effects, which was later to become the keystone of Impressionist philosophy, they used bright colour sparingly, limiting its use to accents within an essentially neutral-coloured whole. It was left to Édouard Manet (1832–83) and Edgar Degas (1834–1917) to question traditional values and explore the use of colour both for its own sake and for the impact it made on the viewer.

Neither was strictly an Impressionist, but both were concerned with depicting the passing moment, both were disenchanted with the generalities of Salon painting and turned to contemporary life for their subject matter. They were separated from the Impressionists by education, social background, artistic aims and age, yet Manet in particular inspired and encouraged the younger Renoir, Monet and Sisley, who became known as his 'gang' – *la bande à Manet*. Manet's shattering of academic doctrine by eliminating middle tones opened

House at Cagnes. Auguste Renoir, 1841-1919
(Ville de Paris, Musée du Petit Palais, Paris)

the way for the true Impressionists to use colour as they wished.

Both Manet and Degas were from upper-middle-class backgrounds, but politically they were poles apart. Degas, a banker's son, was strongly conservative with a love of tradition (he once said of the court of Louis XIV, 'They were dirty perhaps, but distinguished; we are clean but we are common'). Manet was a Republican, whose politics dictated the themes of his pictures (to criticize the policy of Napoleon III in Mexico, he clothed the Mexican firing squad of *The Execution of Maximilian* in French uniform).

Manet had been destined for the navy but failed the necessary examination and entered the studio of Thomas Couture to become a painter. There he rebelled against traditional artistic values. 'Everything we lay our eyes on is ridiculous. The light is wrong, the shadows are wrong. When I come into the studio I feel as if I were entering a tomb.' From the very beginning he defined his goal: 'One must paint one's own times and reproduce what one sees.' He shocked the Salon with his life-size *Absinthe Drinker*, his old teacher, Couture, remarking that there was only one absinthe drinker, 'the painter who produced that piece of madness'. He shocked the public with his *Déjeuner sur l'Herbe* in which a nude girl is represented with two elegantly dressed young men. It echoed a painting by Giorgione, but Manet offended by adopting a contemporary setting rather than a respectable Classical scene.

Manet used watercolour brilliantly in preliminary studies for his paintings, achieving a unity sometimes missing in the finished work. He also produced watercolours which were masterpieces in themselves. *Courses à Longchamp*, painted on the spot in 1864, from which he made a number of oil studies before crystallizing his ideas for the final oil painting, is a fine example. Vibrant blues and greens merge into subtly coloured clouds, the jockeys picked out in red, orange and pink.

Manet first met the young Impressionists, Monet, Pissarro, Sisley, Bazille, Renoir and Cézanne, in 1866. They were immediately attracted to this stimulating, attractive man of the world and became more or less members of Manet's circle, yet they were never seduced by Manet's realism just as Manet, through sharing their influence, never became a true Impressionist.

It was Claude Monet (1840–1926), a poor but determined young man from Le Havre, who took the lead among the emerging Impressionists, urging them to abandon studio painting completely and work *en plein air*, laying every brush stroke directly. His insistence that all paintings of nature should be finished on the spot led him to fit out a small boat as a studio. From this he was able to observe the flickering of light on the water, catch a sunbeam breaking through the clouds, and follow the play of light and shade among the riverside trees. To capture these fleeting images he was forced to evolve new methods: there was no time for mixing colours. These had to be applied in direct touches, juxtaposed to create the sought-after impression and applied at great speed. It was this apparently slapdash treatment that so enraged the critics and Salon painters.

As a young man Monet owed much to Eugène Boudin, who pointed out to him the subtleties of sunlight and reflection; in later life he was to remark, 'It was as if a veil had been removed. The mere example of this artist, devoted to his art and his independent way of life, made me realize what painting could mean.' In 1870, at the outbreak of the Franco-Prussian war, Monet, Pissarro and later Sisley, fled to England to avoid military service. There, strongly influenced by the watercolours of Turner, Crome and Constable, they discovered

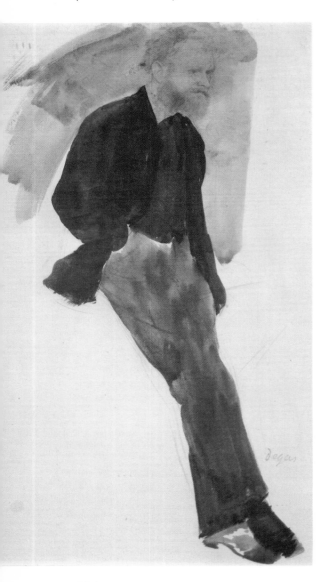

Portrait of Manet. Edgar Degas 1834-1917 (Private Collection)

that the fog and mists of London provided ideal subject matter, and produced some of their finest studies during this self-imposed exile.

Auguste Renoir (1841–1919) also came from an unlikely background for a revolutionary artist, his father being a tailor from Limoges. His *Spring Landscape* of 1877, with its myriad flicks of iridescent colour, represents Impressionism in its fullest form, though Renoir was increasingly drawn to the great Classical tradition of Veronese, Titian, or Velazquez. He said proudly of his masterpiece, *Les Grandes Baigneuses*, 'Rubens would have been satisfied with it.'

Of all the original Impressionists Camille Pissarro (1830–1903) stuck most closely to their ideas. He was the theorist of the movement, and the others looked to him for continuity and direction. For a time he flirted with the *pointilliste* techniques of Seurat and Signac, who juxtaposed dots or points of pigment in the manner of a mosaic to arrive at an overall colour. But he reverted to his original ideals later, and either painted over or destroyed his *pointilliste* work. Like all his fellow Impressionists, he worked fast, averaging at least one painting a week. A kindly, likeable man, he encouraged the new generation, Cézanne, Van Gogh and Gauguin, who wrote of him, 'He was one of my masters, and I do not deny him.'

Alfred Sisley (1839–99), born in Paris of English parents, was another who remained an unwavering Impressionist. He was drawn to the quiet of the countryside for his subject matter, and his paintings reflect his own quiet nature. His best work conveys airiness and a feeling for suffused light, while the vigorous brushwork gives it a sense of controlled energy. His *Regatta at Molesey*, painted during a visit to England, is a dazzling portrayal of a crystal clear summer's day on the River Thames. The clean, astringent blues with flashes of white, the touches of red in the windswept flags, hastily brushed in with bold, well-defined strokes, create a tremendous feeling of space.

Page from Sketchbook. Auguste Renoir
(Louvre, Paris)

A number of lesser artists were at the same time painting in the Impressionist manner or were associated in some way with the movement. Berthe Morisot (1841–95) was introduced to the group by Manet in 1868. She had worked with Corot, a powerful influence who encouraged her to develop a sense of luminosity in her fresh and delicate landscapes. Ignace Fantin-Latour (1836–1904) and Jean-Frédéric Bazille (1841–70) were not true Impressionists and painted somewhat in the style of Manet and the realists. Bazille, like Renoir, enlisted during the Franco-Prussian war; he died in action while serving with the Zouaves. Paul Signac (1863–1935) and Georges Seurat (1859–91) took the movement down a different path. Their *pointilliste*, or 'divisionist' technique had, they claimed, introduced a scientific element into the recording of a passing scene.

Towards the end of the 1870s the Impressionist movement began to lose momentum, and the artists involved split up, both geographically and stylistically. Monet continued to paint as an Impressionist, but he gradually surrendered his original simplicity of concept to introduce 'more serious qualities', as he put it. Renoir had already remarked, 'out of doors one is always cheating.'

Despite their relative lack of material success, the Impressionists fundamentally altered the attitude of many contemporaries towards painting, although sometimes, perhaps, they went too far in attempting to encapsulate an instant in time at the expense of all composition. At the height of their vivid use of colour, even Emile Zola, their fiercest champion, had his doubts. 'Was it for this that I fought – those patches of colour, these reflections, this decomposition of light? Was I mad?'

Three painters of acknowledged genius led the Post-Impressionist movement: Paul Cézanne (1839–1906), Paul Gauguin (1848–1903) and Vincent Van Gogh (1853–90). This trio, while retaining many of the revolutionary ideas of the Impressionists, themselves introduced new discoveries which paved the way for the artistic revolution at the beginning of the 20th century.

At first Cézanne was drawn towards Impressionism, taking part in a number of Impressionist exhibitions. Becoming more and more disgusted with the treatment his paintings received at the hands of the critics, he went home to Aix-en-Provence where, as a man of independent means, he was able to work out his artistic problems far from the hurly burly of Paris and free from the clamour of the critics. Cézanne's concerns were complex. On the one hand he had a passionate desire to paint 'from nature', on the other an equally strong urge to turn Impressionism into 'something more solid and endurable, like the art of the Museums' to restore something of the Classical tradition, to paint 'Poussin from nature'. He was tortured by the exacting standards he set himself, and as the poet Rilke wrote, 'gave himself entirely, his whole strength behind each stroke of the brush. . . He would shake all over, his face heavy with unseen thoughts, his chest sunken, his shoulders hunched, his hands trembling. . .' Cézanne sought to produce 'constructions after nature', an assembly of planes creating solidity and structure.

From 1885 onwards he displayed a special zest for watercolour. He used the medium as a relaxation from oil painting and painted for his own enjoyment pictures never intended for the public eye. His outlook is amusingly summed up in a letter to Émile Zola. 'The picture is not going too badly, but the days seem long. I must buy a box of watercolours so that I can paint when I am not working on my picture'. Cézanne's colour is subdued, discreet, with lavish use of the reflective surface of the white paper. In his *Mont Sainte-Victoire*, painted towards the end of his life, the careful brush strokes of delicate blue, violet, yellow, pink and green combine with the white areas to suggest structure and to create a feeling of light and space.

Entirely different to Cézanne, less intellectual and more instinctive, Vincent Van Gogh used rich colour and form to transmit his feelings for things. With no time for 'stereoscopic reality', as he called it, he would not hesitate to distort objects if it helped to express what he felt, whereas Cézanne, using only as much correct perspective as he considered necessary, explored the relationships of colour and form. Van Gogh's intensity of vision can be glimpsed in his verbal description of the simple lodgings he had at Arles: 'The walls are pale violet. The ground is of red tiles. The wood of the bed and chairs is the yellow of fresh butter, the sheets and pillows very light greenish lemon. The coverlet scarlet. The window green. The toilet table orange, the basin blue. The doors lilac.'

Van Gogh came into contact with the Impressionists in 1886, when he was thirty-three. For years he had been struggling to express himself as an artist, with indifferent success. He was torn between painting and religion and had been engaged in missionary work among Belgian coalminers until dismissed for 'excess of zeal'. He made his own clothes, slept rough and gave everything he had to the poor.

Through the Impressionists he discovered the bustle of Paris life which he painted in a near frenzy of vivid colour. The immense strain under which he worked, the feverish pace he set himself, proved too much: he broke down and was confined to a mental asylum in 1889. He continued to paint until he committed suicide in 1891. Pissarro, the painter who exerted most influence on Van Gogh, maintained that the first time he clapped eyes on him, 'I knew he would either go mad or surpass us all. But I did not know he would do both.'

When living at Arles Van Gogh, hungry for companionship and dreaming of an artistic brotherhood, invited another late starter, Paul Gauguin, to join him at Arles. Gauguin was a stockbroker who had left his wife and children after twelve years of marriage to become a painter. He had none of Van Gogh's humility, in fact he was self-confident to the point of arrogance, but he was sickened by the

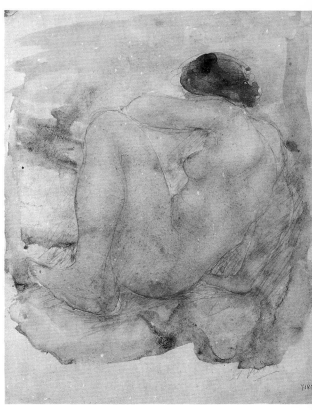

Above: *Nude*. Auguste Rodin, 1840-1917 (Musée Rodin, Paris)

Left: *Trees and Houses*. Paul Cézanne, 1839-1906 (Museum Boymans-van Beuningen, Rotterdam)

Two views of Mont Sainte-Victoire by Paul Cézanne (Above National Gallery of Ireland, Dublin; below Tate Gallery, London)

slickness and superficiality of contemporary art. A painter, he believed, should probe deeper into what he called 'the mysterious centre of the mind'. The companionship of two such different characters, despite mutual artistic admiration, was doomed to failure. Two years later Gauguin left for Tahiti, in search of a simple life which would allow him to develop his art in the direction he chose.

Gauguin's watercolours are powerfully expressive, immensely strong in colour and pattern. He habitually used sumptuous colour, nowhere more than in his rare watercolour studies of flowers, where rich reds, deep violets, orange, gold and pinks vie with each other in an iridescent glow.

37

The Ferment of the New

Following the Impressionist revolution, a small number of painters were left with a feeling of emptiness. While absorbing the lessons taught by the movement, they felt an unease at its superficiality, and a desire to go beyond a preoccupation with the fleeting moment and an exploration of the optical qualities of light. Cézanne, Gauguin and Van Gogh set the ball rolling. Their dissatisfaction with the direction in which painting was heading was to have a profound effect on many emerging young artists. It was this dissatisfaction which triggered off those experiments at the turn of the century that led to the birth of what we know as modern art.

Cézanne's preoccupation with balance and form paved the way for Picasso and Cubism; Van Gogh's rendering of his intense feelings for Expressionism, and Gauguin's striving for direct simplicity to the various aspects of Primitivism. The stage was set for the appearance of the seemingly lunatic movements that so startled and shocked both the art world and the public. Meanwhile, there were artists still painting in the manner of the Impressionists, particularly in countries that had not readily accepted the aims of the movement. There were also many, many artists still following the traditional principles of the academies.

That artists should strive to express themselves rather than offer a faithful portrayal of their natural surroundings was not by any means a new concept. Medieval art had been formalized to express the glory of God; Egyptian painting aimed to convey information, the artist setting down 'fact' rather than appearance; the Chinese sought to capture the spirit or essence of their subject. It was not until the Renaissance that the artist was urged to paint what he saw. The generation that followed the Impressionists attempted to convey to the viewer what they felt about their subject, and they distorted form, colour and content in an effort to express an idea. This search for greater depth, under the shadowy and often misleading term

Overleaf: *Odalisque*. Georges Rouault, 1871-1958 (Private Collection)

Below left: A fanciful 'inner-eye' treatment of butterflies and flowers by Odilon Redon, 1840-1916 (Ville de Paris, Musée du Petit Palais, Paris)

Below: *Grande décoration au masque*, 1923. Henri Matisse (Private Collection, Paris)

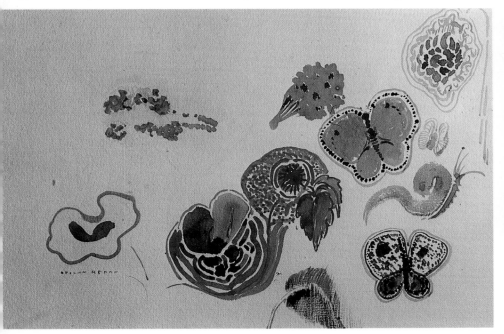

Right: *Notre Dame*. Henri Matisse, 1869-1954 (Private Collection)

'Expressionism' – the effort to depict the artist's inner vision – was summed up by Van Gogh. Writing of how he set about painting a portrait of a dear friend, he began, 'I exaggerate the fair colour of the hair, I take orange, chrome, lemon colour, and behind the head I do not paint the trivial wall of the room but the Infinite. I make a simple background out of the most intense and richest blue the palette will yield. The blond luminous head stands out against this strong blue background mysteriously like a star in the azure. Alas, my dear friend, the public will see nothing but caricature in this exaggeration, but what does that matter to us?'

The new movements – Expressionism, Cubism, Futurism – blossomed. The *Fauves* 'wild beasts', headed by Henri Matisse, to whom the label is absurdly inappropriate, appeared on the Parisian scene. Often the aims of artists overlapped: Picasso, founder of Cubism, painted a frankly Expressionist watercolour in *Brooding Woman*, and the Fauves exhibited at the Berlin *Secession* exhibition of 1911. The term Expressionist was coined at this exhibition, and although the movement later became associated with German artists, in the first instance it was used to denote a group of mainly French artists, exhibiting in a different hall – Vlamink, Derain, Picasso, Marquet, Van Dongen, Puy and Manquin. The reaction from some

Opposite: *Still-life with Bottle,* 1913. Georges Braque, 1882-1963 (Private Collection)

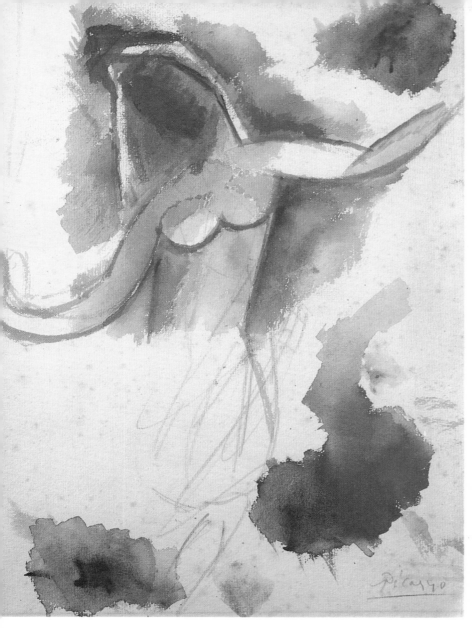

Left: Study for *Les Demoiselles d'Avignon*, 1906. Pablo Picasso (Private Collection, Berne)

Below: *Portrait of a Young Man*, 1900. Pablo Picasso (Private Collection)

quarters was immediate and bitter. One critic, after referring to the 'clowning' of a few French artists, went on to castigate the German painters of the movement: 'They apparently think they can impress the German public by calling upon their Paris prototypes as evidence of the fact that they are not lagging behind the most modern of the French.'

For all that, Expressionism found fallow ground in Germany, appealing to the national mysticism previously evident in the work of the Nazarenes. But it infuriated the 'little man', the *bourgeois*, shocking him out of his complacency by presenting him, not with idealized beauty, but stark reality as the artist saw it. It also fell foul of the growing National Socialist Party, which when it came to power in 1933, banned virtually all modern art. Many artists, forbidden to work, chose to go into exile.

An artist who explored the possibilities of Expressionism in psychological depth was the Norwegian Edvard Munch (1863–1944).

His disturbing pictures plumbed emotions unconnected with aesthetic 'beauty' in the traditional sense. It was this move by painters to express 'ugliness' and anguish that critic and public resented. If artists had to change what they saw, they should make it ideally beautiful and pleasing – so the Philistines said.

Watercolour took on new meanings in the hands of the Expressionists. It became an inquiry into visual relationships that ranged from the free calligraphy of Kandinsky at one end of the spectrum, to the controlled pictorial forms of Paul Klee at the other. Artists drawn to the act of handwriting – to a greater or lesser degree – to express themselves, included Kandinsky, Nolde, Derain, Kokoshka, Picasso and Rouault. Among those controlling the spontaneous immediacy of the medium to construct finished pictures were Marc Chagall, Klee again, Egon Schiele, Max Ernst and Maurice de Vlamink.

In Paris the Fauves indulged in pattern making and the use of vibrant colour, totally discarding the study of natural form. The most important figure in this group, Henri Matisse, who was to have such a marked effect on modern design, studied the colour schemes of Oriental textiles and scenery to arrive at his sensuous patterns. The Cubists, headed by Picasso, Braque and Juan Gris, took Cézanne's treatment of form a stage further, constructing pictures along what might be caused the Egyptian principle, breaking down the object into planes to depict each element from its most characteristic angle. The modern watercolour has grown out of this seething era of inquiry and experiment, with today's artists still seeking to make it the vehicle of a unique personal form.

The Absinthe Drinker. Marc Chagall (Private Collection)

38

British Watercolours in the 20th Century

The English watercolour school, which flourished for more than a century, reached its height in the splendid Romantic landscapes of Turner, Cotman, Constable, Cox, de Wint, Bonington and others; in the mystical, often disturbing work of Blake and the rich orchards of Samuel Palmer. After 1850, however this vigorous national art form degenerated into one of technical virtuosity and prettiness. The broad controlled washes of Cotman, the 'flittering light' of Turner, gave way to the fussy stipple of Birket Foster's cloying rural scenes – although at times, particularly in his seascapes, there is a glimmer of what might have been. Towards the end of the century, more and more artists turned to watercolour as a medium, but in general they slipped into sentimentality, using over-bright colours in an attempt to ape oil painting. Landscape as an art had lost its momentum.

The Pre-Raphaelites had made a valiant effort to stem the ebbing tide with a return to earlier, more precise values, but their movement, too consciously medieval, petered out. A second wave of enthusiasts led by Burne-Jones, Watts, Leighton and Poynter, prints from whose work became the delight of seaside landladies, did little to revitalize watercolour which by the turn of the century had drifted into the sterile orientalism of Alma-Tadema or the hot-house eroticism of Aubrey Beardsley.

The beginning of the 20th century saw a dramatic break with the immediate past. Watercolour took on a fresh impetus; new ideas, championed by Roger Fry, flooded into Britain from the Post-Impressionists and the Fauves. Many British artists were also discovering the standards of English landscape which had flourished a century before. The time was ripe for the renewal which began with the foundation of the New English Art Club in 1886.

Founded to shake the Royal Academy out of its lethargic

Below left: *Farmyard.* Philip Wilson Steer (Tate Gallery, London)

Below: *Margaret Nash, the Artist's Wife.* Paul Nash, 1899-1946 (Victoria and Albert Museum, London)

Chapel in the Park. David Jones (Tate Gallery, London)

complacency, the New English Art Club was the vanguard of the revival. In the work of Wilson Steer (1860–1942), a founder member, the tradition of the 19th-century landscape watercolourists was revived; many of his paintings suggest John Sell Cotman in their control of flat washes. Steer was basically a traditionalist with a love of the countryside, to which he brought his own brand of atmospheric awareness; solid forms melt away in a haze of sunlight or mist. His colour is calm and restrained, at times close to monochrome.

Born in Denmark, Walter Richard Sickert (1860–1942), another early member of the New English Art Club, settled in England and became more British than the British. He shared with Degas and Toulouse-Lautrec a passion for the theatre, in particular the music hall, and much of his best work is devoted to that theme and to low life in the more sordid areas of London.

Another painter of the early 20th century using watercolour in the

English Romantic tradition was Alfred Thornton (*d*1939), who evoked much of Samuel Palmer's vision in his landscapes, relying very much on dramatic light and shade. The Welsh artist Sir Frank Brangwyn (1867–1956), developed a freedom of style and a predilection for rich colour and voluptuous form. Combining watercolour with gouache, he produced a seemingly endless stream of designs for murals, covering vast areas with exotic fruit, flowers and foliage. Christopher Nevinson (1889–1946) and Augustus John are remembered for their poignant watercolours in the First World War; John's paintings of gypsies are especially close to the tradition of British Romanticism.

Duncan Grant (1885–1978) and Sir Matthew Smith (1879–1959) were inspired by the Fauves, Grant in particular emulating their startling contrasts of hot and cold colour, but only Wyndham Lewis (1884–1957) threw himself unreservedly into the continental movements. Caught up in the ferment of those stirring days before

At the Seaside, 1913. Percy Wyndham Lewis, 1884-1957 (Victoria and Albert Museum, London)

241

1914, he launched the Vorticist movement, which was his own personal interpretation of Cubism.

One of the major watercolour artists to emerge in this century was Paul Nash (1889–1946). Also blooded during the First World War, he made a number of telling studies of the Western Front which did a lot to stimulate an emotional violence but later turned to a dreamlike involvement with romantic landscape. Nash's dream world, which he seemed to be able to enter at will, echoes the visual imagery of Blake and Palmer. His use of dominant foreground shapes – whether they be megaliths, plant forms or crashed Dornier bombers – against haunting skies with Blake-like suns and moons, marks Nash as a complete Romantic in the mainstream tradition.

David Jones (1895–1974) blossomed as a watercolourist with a natural gift for linear pattern, his ethereal pictures, made up of delicate, fragile colours, washed over a wiry pencil line. His work reflects the quiet, contemplative side of the national heritage, finely tuned, semireligious; a far cry from that of Graham Sutherland (1903–80) and John Piper (b1903). Sutherland was influenced by Samuel Palmer from an early stage, an influence coupled with a strange disquiet that owed much to Blake. Piper, another neo-Romantic, though more theatrical in his approach than Sutherland, also owed a debt to the early English Romantics and indeed the topographers. His rich texture and vibrant colour made his work eminently suitable for theatre design and stained glass.

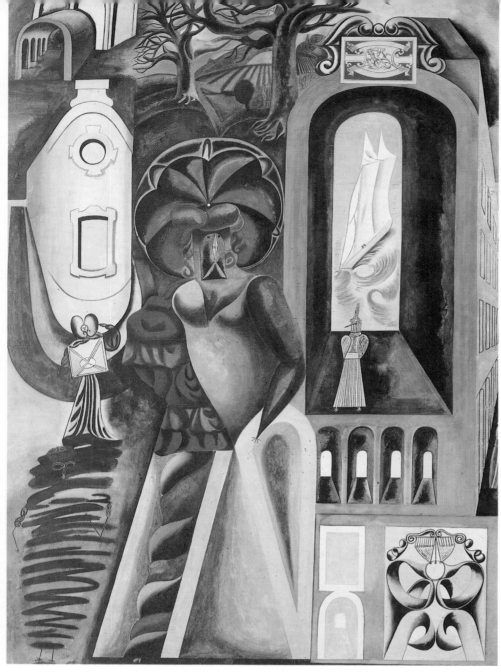

Opposite top: *The Wanderer II,* 1940.
Graham Sutherland, 1903-1980 (Victoria and
Albert Museum, London)

Opposite bottom: *Valley and River,
Northumberland.* Edward Burra, 1905-1976
(Tate Gallery, London)

Left: *Surrealist Composition, c.*1934. Edward
Burra (Victoria and Albert Museum,
London)

Other artists who exploited watercolour to express an individual
viewpoint were Edward Burra, whose large, livid watercolours of the
Second World War exude feelings of the tragedy of war, a feeling also
apparent in the highly textured, surrealist figures of Henry Moore.
Albert Richards, Edward Bawden and Eric Ravilious were all polished
watercolourists, and Ivon Hitchins's splendidly coloured studies,
though non figurative, have all the emotion of the neo-Romantic
school.

Among other recent artists who used watercolour either for studies
or picture making were John Minton, Francis Bacon, Graham Bell,
Lucien Freud, Ben Nicholson, Victor Passmore and Ethel Walker.
Although the search for new expression in watercolour has, in the
main, switched to the United States, a number of young artists in
Britain are still experimenting in the medium.

Parallel to the developing neo-Romantic school, there has been
since the beginning of the century, a continuous flow of more
naturalistic watercolours aimed largely at the print market.
Topographical landscapes still abound, and satisfy a popular demand.
Notable among these artists was Sir William Russell Flint (1880–1969)
whose work was lifted from the mundane by striking technical
dexterity, for instance in the control of washes and conscious
granulation of colour (his equipment also included a bunsen burner
and sponge), not to mention his cultivated eroticism.

Overleaf: *Somerset Place, Bath,* 1942. John
Piper (Tate Gallery, London)

243

Watercolour Now

Since the Second World War artists, particularly those working in watercolour, have formalized ideas and concepts in the search for graphic interpretation of natural form. Many of the 'modern masters' who had come to the fore at the beginning of the century continued to work in Paris, using watercolour: Picasso, Matisse, Braque, Rouault and others. Some returned to Paris from voluntary exile in America (Léger, Chagall, Ernst, etc.) The remainder stayed to paint in the country of their adoption, Kokoshka in England, Hans Hofmann, Beckmann and Tanguy in the United States. They, together with Sutherland, Dufy, Piper, Tobey, Kline, Dubuffet, Pollock and Feininger, in their own countries, set the pattern that was to have such an influence on the rising generation of artists still working today.

No longer restricted by conventional taboos, the taste of patrons

Right: *Untitled.* Sam Francis (National Museum of American Art, Smithsonian Institution, Washington, D.C. Gift of Mr and Mrs David Anderson - Martha Jackson Memorial Collection)

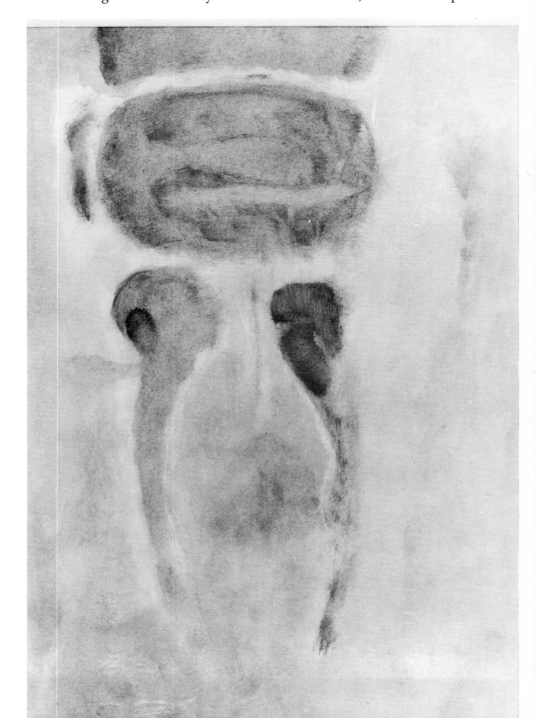

Opposite: *Painting.* Sam Francis (Tate Gallery, London)

Opposite: *Peddler, c.*1930-1935. Jackson Pollock (National Museum of American Art, Smithsonian Institution, Washington, D.C. Gift of Thomas Hart Benton)

Right: *Interior of the Studio,* 1937. Mark Tobey, 1890–1976 (National Gallery of Art, Washington D.C. Gift of Ambrose and Viola Patterson, 1978)

Below: *Gouache.* Mark Tobey (Galérie Pauli, Lausanne)

or religious conventions, the artist of today is free to explore visual phenomena unhindered, wandering down any path that takes his fancy. Never before has there been greater scope for experiment. But are the results comparable with Turner or Constable? Many people believe not and are convinced that social restrictions are necessary for great art. Yet in his day Turner had many and violent critics, and fifty years were to elapse after the death of Constable before the genius of his watercolours was recognized.

Abstract Expressionism, *Tachisme*, Drip and Action painting have introduced calligraphic, abstract imagery. Concepts of space and form,

Opposite top: Study for *The Studio*. John Winslow (In the Collection of the Corcoran Gallery of Art, Washington. D.C. Gift of The Women's Committee)

Right: *Catalina Island*. Edward Reep (National Museum of American Art, Smithsonian Institution, Washington. D.C. Gift of the Ford Motor Company)

Right: Study for *Sleeping King Ascending*. Robert Stackhouse (In the Collection of the Corcoran Gallery of Art, Washington, D.C. Museum Purchase with funds from the National Endowment for the Arts, the William A. Clark Fund, and Margaret M. Hitchcock)

the 'ever-opening line', have been explored by Jackson Pollock and others. Here the eye is not asked to focus on a single element but encouraged to wander at will through a composition. Following from Klee, Kandinsky, Miró, Picasso and Matisse, the modern watercolourist strives to see beyond the obvious; blots, grotesque forms and slashing lines are employed in the attempt to release

individual interpretation. Strangely enough, through all the myriad styles and conceits, there emerges yet a pervading romanticism.

New names rise constantly to the fore, each artist concerned with his own visual world: Jack Kling, Glen Bradshaw, John McIvor, Irene Koch, Sam Francis, Corneille, Mathieu, Oldenburg, Paolozzi, Rauschenberg, and numerous others.

Below: *Dale City (Virginia),* 1978. Val Lewton (In the Collection of the Corcoran Gallery of Art, Washington, D.C. Gift of The Women's Committee)

251

Glossary

Barbizon school: a group of French landscape painters in the 19th century who took their name from the village near the Forest of Fontainebleau where most of them lived for a time from the 1830s. Their goal was to paint nature as seen, and they were opposed to current academic theory. Stemming from the Romantic movement, they were influenced by English painters, especially Bonington.

Baroque: a name applied to the style or period in European art which followed the purer Classicism of the Renaissance; reaching its peak in the 17th century. It was in general grander, more dramatic, even theatrical, though still based on Classical principles to a great extent.

Body colour: watercolour mixed with white to make it opaque, and therefore identical with gouache; used to emphasize highlights or areas of local colour by artists such as Turner to great effect.

Chiaroscuro: the method of treating light and dark in a painting; used to relate one object to another or to heighten dramatic effect; a special feature of the work of many Baroque painters.

Classical: in the style of ancient Greece and Rome, but in painting more particularly this style as filtered through the art of the Renaissance. Some painters adopted Classical subjects without embracing a Classical style, the essence of which is the pursuit of the ideal and in painting tends to be linear, 'hard' and restrained in colour.

Distemper: nowadays a term associated more with house paint than high art; the pigment is bound with size, a method used by the ancient Egyptians and the Greeks. See *tempera*.

Fresco: a method of painting a wall (or ceiling etc.) while the plaster is still wet, or fresh (*fresco*). See Chapter 11.

Gothic: a rather wide term which embraces several centuries of European art, from the 12th century to the Renaissance; Gothic painting is mainly though not exclusively confined to illuminated manuscripts, and displays a greater richness, more delight in nature and the individual, and brighter colours than the preceding Romanesque period.

Gouache: opaque watercolour, obtained by mixing Chinese white with ordinary watercolour pigments. It was the usual method employed by medieval illuminators and was popular with continental watercolorists in the 18th century, and modern American artists.

Illusionism: in painting, the creation of a pictorial illusion of reality. Most figurative painting is illusionist to an extent, but the term is applied particularly to work in which the attempt to suggest three dimensions is a dominant motive.

Local colour: the actual, 'real' colour of any object, unaffected by reflection of light or of any other neighbouring colour.

Picturesque: More specifically than the obvious general meaning ('like a picture'), the term is applied to a deliberately cultivated charm in a painting, particularly a landscape. Though often used as a term of opprobrium, there was a vogue for the picturesque in Romantic painting which was not necessarily sugary or sentimental.

Romanesque: the style of art in Europe in the 11th and 12th centuries, mainly confined to sculpture and architecture; in Romanesque painting the most striking characteristic is the use of rhythmical, abstract designs.

Romantic: in art history this word is applied in particular to the general cultural movement of the late 18th century characterized by emotional release, a love of landscape, especially wild landscape, and a predilection for anything exotic, weird or mysterious – all features of a greater individual freedom of expression. Of course, 'romantic' aspects may be detected in the art of practically any era.

Sinopia: a reddish-brown, earthy colour often used in the underdrawing of a fresco, and hence applied to the drawing itself.

Tempera: an early painting medium, used in ancient times and throughout the Middle Ages, into the Renaissance. The pigment is ground and bound with (usually) egg, especially the yolk. It is soluble in water but lasting, as well as quick-drying, which meant that painters had to work fairly fast.

Topographical: this term is applied to the work of certain landscape painters, of the 18th century mainly, which aimed at an objective, faithful reproduction of a scene; view painting is another word for this type of work, and it has close affinities with *veduta*, 'a landscape portrayed precisely and recognizably . . . a historically objective landscape'.

Index

Figures in italics refer to illustrations

253